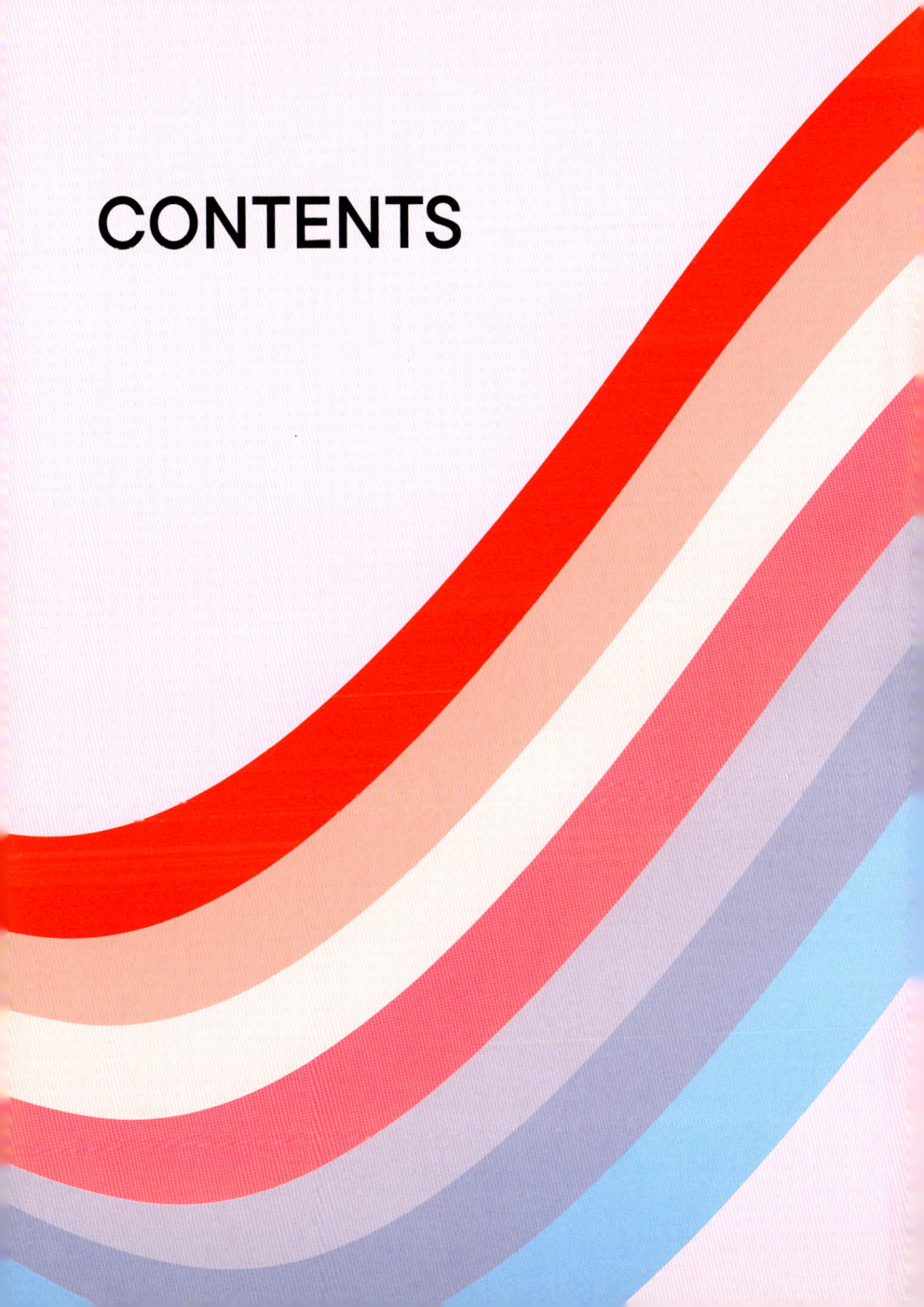

CONTENTS

Natalie
Hammond

STYLE CODES

Dolly
Parton

Abrams, New York

STYLE CODES

Dolly Parton

"We're all unique,
but she's more unique
than anyone else."

JANE FONDA

*I*n March 1983, aged thirty-seven and at the height of her fame, Dolly Parton touched down at London's Heathrow Airport. An HBO special, *Dolly in London*, was filmed to document her journey from the airport to a very special concert that was taking place in the heart of London's West End. The documentary's opening scene showed Dolly, her curled wig surprisingly buoyant despite the long-haul flight, going through passport control. For the trip, Dolly had poured her petite frame into a strawberry-red ensemble that stood out next to the square gray suit of the man asking about the reason for her visit. The other travelers in baggage claim also looked decidedly stale in comparison—Dolly was a mirage. It was like she had arrived from an entirely different world, which, in a way, she had.

The documentary's first few minutes were dedicated to a series of scenes that showed Dolly, America's country music queen, being whisked around on a whistle-stop tour of

London, taking in postcard snapshots of the city's most famous monuments. After singing with the so-called Pearly Kings and Queens, strumming her banjo to the crowds in Covent Garden, Dolly emerged in beaded regalia from a double-decker bus and, flanked by two rows of Beefeater—the iconic guards of the Tower of London, with their primary red uniforms and tall "bearskin" hats—she made her way to the venue through overjoyed crowds.

Halfway through the concert, she changed, shimmying back onto the stage wearing a magnificently sequinned dress by the Western Costume Company, one that swooped down at the neck, up at the thigh, and whittled the singer's already itty-bitty waist with its oh-so-spangled belt. At a press conference shown earlier in the program, a journalist asked her why country music had such a fan base in the UK. Dolly replied, "I think country music tells real stories about real people, very ordinary stories. I'd like to think, in my case, told in an extraordinary way," then she laughed at her own little joke. The same reasoning could be used to explain the way she has always dressed—which is also extraordinary.

In 1983, Dolly Parton was a woman at the pinnacle of her success. She had released twenty-four solo albums and, with two box office hits under her belt, she had also broken into Hollywood. With stirring country music anthems like "Just Because I'm a Woman" (1968), "Jolene" (1973), and "I Will Always Love You" (1974), which was famously covered by Whitney Houston, Dolly had made her mark as a prodigious songwriting talent, as well as the angelic soprano of East Tennessee. She had come a long way from the Great Smoky Mountains.

As the fourth of twelve children, she had grown up with very little in the way of material possessions, but she'd had a lot of dreams—and even more grit. By the age of ten, Dolly was singing on local radio stations in Knoxville.

By twenty-one, she had filled the regular "girl singer" slot on *The Porter Wagoner Show*. The American TV institution was hosted by the rhinestone-wearing, pompadour-sporting showman Porter Wagoner, and was hugely popular with country music enthusiasts. Dolly did all this while wearing her distinctive bold outfits and big hair—a look that she had been cultivating since leaving home for Nashville. For Dolly, it was this gig that led to a life-changing record contract with the influential label RCA.

Dolly is one of the most decorated performers of all time—she's been inducted into the Country Music Hall of Fame (1999), the Songwriters Hall of Fame (2001), and the Rock & Roll Hall of Fame (2022)—but she is also widely celebrated for her philanthropic work with the Imagination Library, a childhood-literacy scheme that, as of February 2024, has put 229 million free books into the hands of young readers around the world.

Despite her having a career that has already spanned more than half a century (and shows no signs of stopping anytime soon), it is amazing to see that the cornerstones of Dolly Parton's spectacular wardrobe haven't changed all that much over the decades. She still wears bold outfits, and her blonde hair is still impeccably coiffed to add extra height.

For as long as she can remember, people have been trying to persuade Dolly to get rid of her outrageous wigs and her distracting clothes, but, always true to herself, she has never relented. She fought to preserve her distinctive look, and fought to stop it from being picked apart, rhinestone by rhinestone, by people who wanted her to change in order to fit in. Fitting in was never Dolly's modus operandi—she always wanted to stand out.

She has recently released a coffee-table book, *Behind the Seams: My Life in Rhinestones*, a shimmering encyclopedia that documents

Dolly's life as a fashion icon (although that's not a term she has ever agreed is a fitting one). As she writes, "It makes me laugh when people call me a fashion icon. I always say I'm more like an eyesore, because it never, ever crossed my mind to be fashionable—and I never was fashionable. As long as I'm comfortable in what I'm wearing and I think it looks good on me, then that's my fashion. That's my style."

Style Codes: Dolly Parton will take you on a journey through the enduring hallmarks of the singer's unique style and fashion choices. If you learn only one rule of style from Dolly, let it be this: Never wear something that doesn't make you feel like you.

WEAR A RAINBOW OF COLOR

"When someone shows you their true colors, believe them."

DOLLY PARTON

STYLE CODES: DOLLY PARTON

*D*olly Parton has one of the sunniest personalities in showbiz, so it's no surprise that she gravitates toward color. In fact, one of her most famous childhood anecdotes is about her so-called coat of many colors—the very item that went on to inspire one of her most memorable songs of the seventies. Dolly's mother, Avie Lee Parton, used to make her children "new" clothes out of old scraps, and when she noticed that her fourth child loved different colors, she saved up the swatches until she had enough of an assortment to make Dolly a patchwork coat for school; Dolly was beside herself with excitement when it was finished. The only problem was that her schoolmates teased her mercilessly about the homemade coat, and as the ribbing escalated, the children even went as far as to shut Dolly in a cupboard. The joke was on them, of course, as an illustration of Dolly as a child, wearing the coat, went on to be the cover of her eighth album, also named *Coat of Many Colors* (1971).

Not only does Dolly still wear multiple colors, but she has also had several of her designer friends make replicas of the original coat. A tuxedo jacket made of intersecting rainbow diamonds, worn at 2016's Academy of Country Music Awards, was certainly a fitting tribute to her mother's creation.

From the start of her career on *The Porter Wagoner Show*, which began in 1967, Dolly's wardrobe contained a rainbow of colors. According to Stephen Miller's biography of the singer, *Smart Blonde*, at the height of its success, *The Porter Wagoner Show* had a viewership of 4 million people a week, and featured Wagoner, his band—the Wagonmasters—and a "girl singer" to act as his counterpart. Dolly filled the slot of "girl singer" after it was vacated by Norma Jean, a famous country music singer from Oklahoma. As well as having to win over audiences who were initially steadfast in their loyalty to Jean, Dolly also had to sing jingles for less than glamorous products made by the show's advertiser, the Chattanooga Medicine Company. To dress the part, Dolly often wore outfits that coordinated with Wagoner's. Wagoner was famous for his suits—flush with country swagger—that were made by Nudie Cohn. He wore them religiously for the covers of his and Dolly's duet albums that were released by RCA, the record company they shared, which were made to capitalize on their on-screen chemistry as the seasoned country star and the ingénue. Although she'd appeared many times on the radio and had performed at the motherland of country music itself, the Grand Ole Opry, this was her first gig as a regular. In Nashville, Dolly was figuring out what she liked and what she didn't like to wear, and was learning how to dress for the stage with help from her then designer, Lucy Adams. What they landed on was a formula that would last for the entirety of Dolly's career: bright colors, big hair, and plenty of sparkle.

We'll come to the hair and the sparkle in good time, but for now, let's talk color. Dolly has worn every shade under the sun—from soft pastels to somewhat punchier primaries—so you're really spoiled for choice. Some of her most eye-catching color choices have been canary, emerald, lime, tangerine, and vermillion. But if you had to isolate three colors that stand out as being particularly "Dolly," it would have to be pink, red, and, interestingly, white. Dolly has even gone on the record to say that her favorite color is one that people don't even think of as being a color at all. White is a rather overlooked neutral that's usually associated with undershirts, underwear, and shirting—in other words, the basics. Well, there's nothing basic about white when it's worn by Dolly.

If you want a shortcut to instantly looking a little more Dolly, wear one of these colors head to toe for twice the impact. Remember: Less is never more when it comes to Dolly.

DOLLY'S RAINBOW THROUGHOUT THE YEARS

1946 – 1956

GIRLHOOD IN THE GREAT SMOKY MOUNTAINS

Dolly's "coat of many colors" was made of whatever scraps of fabric her mother had on hand (from the illustration on the cover of her single "Coat of Many Colors" (1971), it looks like the hues were mostly blue and brown).

1967-1974

THE PORTER WAGONER SHOW

Dolly wore peppy colors as the "girl singer" on *The Porter Wagoner Show*, as well as jewel tones that looked sumptuous on-screen.

1978

HEARTBREAKER

Pastel pink is a color often worn by Dolly, but it first appeared on her *Heartbreaker* album cover in 1978, when she wore a ruffled pink dress. The dress lived up to the album's name—with one of her legs propped up, Dolly showed quite a stretch of thigh in the photo.

1980

9 TO 5

With outfits designed by Ann Roth, Dolly Parton's tenacious character in *9 to 5*, Doralee, wore secretary-appropriate clothes in a palette of butter-wouldn't-melt hues.

THE HOLLYWOOD YEARS

As Hollywood came calling, Dolly's wardrobe shone as bright as a star thanks to the designs of Tony Chase.

the eighties

1986

THE DOLLYWOOD YEARS

The Dollywood theme park opened in the eighties, and Dolly, ever the game proprietor, would often appear wearing suitably fun costumes to wave to the thousands-strong crowds.

HUNGRY AGAIN

Dolly stripped everything back for 1998's *Hungry Again*—her thirty-fifth album—wearing denim overalls.

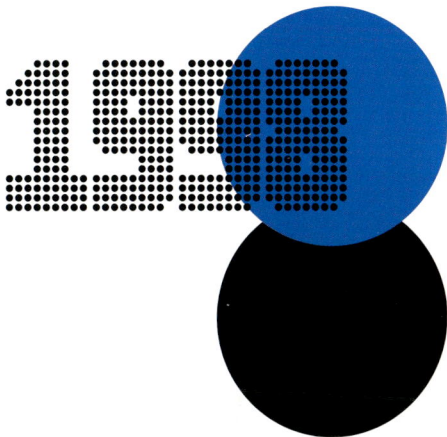

1998

2008

BACKWOODS BARBIE

Ten years later, Dolly was still wearing every shade under the sun, including the punchiest hot pink for 2008's *Backwoods Barbie*.

ROBÉRT BEHAR

The Paris-born, Los Angeles–based costume designer Robért Behar created some wonderfully colorful looks for Dolly—as well as some of her most iconic, including the magnificent white gown she wore to the 2006 Kennedy Center Honors ceremony, which shimmered with swathes of pearls, rhinestones, and silvery beads. The pair met in 1996 through Sandy Gallin, Dolly's incredibly well-connected manager. Behar immediately got the measure of his new client's larger-than-life personal style—especially when it came to color, and over their time together, he designed her a rainbow of looks, using colors such as fuchsia pink and flame orange. He also shared a sense of playfulness with Dolly, designing her a "stars and stripes" outfit for the cover of her fourtieth solo album, *For God and Country* (2003), the image from which was eventually blown up and painted on the nose of a plane belonging to the US Air Force.

HOW TO WEAR PRIMARY

Dolly has worn a lot of reds over the years, but her favorite shade is primary red—the same color as her lacquered nails. It's fabulous and feisty—no one should mess with a person wearing red—and it has made many of her outfits much more memorable. Primary red was the color she was wearing when she first met her husband, Carl Dean, on the street outside the Wishy Washy laundromat in Nashville (no wonder she caught his eye as he drove), and it was also a color that she frequently chose for the covers of her shared albums with Porter Wagoner, most notably their very first, *Just Between You and Me*, where they're both in casual mode wearing cozy primary red turtleneck sweaters. Later in her career, it was the shade chosen for some of her most dramatic looks, like the stupendous red gown designed by Theadora Van Runkle. Dolly wore the gown in her second film, *The Best Little Whorehouse in Texas* (the movie version of the musical hit, released in 1982), which had fiery ruffles erupting at either shoulder and flame-like beading from shoulder to ankle.

RED

Anyone can wear primary red—it's one of those shades that flatters any skin tone and, just as importantly, any style preference. At the most immersive end of the scale, you've got sizzling red dresses—and trust me, they'll always be sizzling if they're primary red—which are such an easy yet impactful way to introduce chilli-pepper red into your rotation. If you're unsure, a good way to develop your working relationship with primary red is to try it first as a crewneck or turtleneck sweater. It'll add polish, not to mention a pop, to ordinary beige slacks or a gray wool skirt—minimal fuss, maximum impact. Another way to come to grips with this color is through accessories. A primary red shoulder bag will lift anything that you wear it with, ditto for red ankle boots (which look particularly good with denim), red ballet flats, and, at the more casual end of the spectrum, a red baseball cap.

If you're still not convinced that it's your color, paint your nails with a primary red polish. Now, run your manicured hand along the clothes hanging in your wardrobe and you'll start to notice that this shade goes with almost everything, from brown to green, pink to black, white to yellow. Give it a go.

"My favorite color is a no color. It's white. I love to wear white when I'm performing onstage. It just makes me feel all light and airy," Dolly said in a video interview with *Wired*. If you feel nervous about the prospect of wearing head-to-toe white right off the bat—not just because of how vigilant you'll have to be at lunchtime, but also because of its sheer "look-at-me" factor—remember that it's a "no color," a neutral.

Some of the world's chicest women from all walks of life—those in pop, rock, politics, and even the royal family—have sworn by head-to-toe white, including Cher, Madonna, Michelle Obama, and Princess Diana, so it's time to get past the idea that it's "too much," because there's no such thing in the world of Dolly. Also, you don't have to wear a glimmering white gown that positively dazzles anyone who looks your way. Why not start with something easy like white jeans with a white T-shirt? Just make sure your jeans are wide-legged—skinny is verging on a no-no in this particular scenario, sorry—and tuck your tee into the jeans' waistband. It's kind of a "nothing" outfit that nonetheless looks incredibly chic, especially if you add some white sunglasses.

For something smarter still, try suiting, although a two-piece with shorts is much cooler than pants, which tend to look a little "politician" in my opinion. Bermuda-length shorts, on the other hand, give the whole outfit a more relaxed mood. Stock up on a good stain remover and you're good to go.

HOW TO FEEL CONFIDENT IN HEAD-TO-TOE WHITE

"What would Dolly do
if someone told her
she should tone down
her style?"

KELLEIGH BANNEN

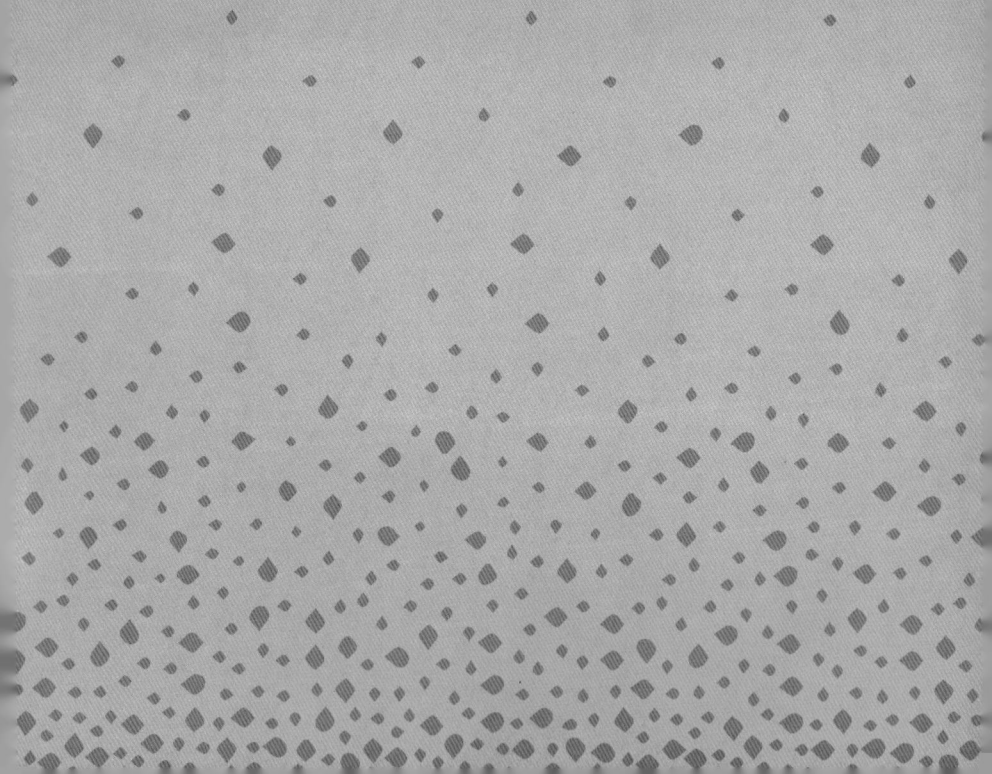

"I'd say go to hell,
I ain't doing it."

DOLLY PARTON

HOW TO PICK YOUR SHADE OF PINK

Pink is important to the persona of Dolly. At least, that's the only conclusion you can draw once you realize that it's the color she chose for so many of her most significant outfits.

The year was 1968. And to collect her very first Country Music Association Award, Dolly glided to the winner's podium wearing a chiffon gown the color of cotton candy. It was just as sweet and airy, too, with an embellished collar that would also become something of a signature. In fact, a very similar pink would be the shade she chose for another "first." In 1980, Dolly made a seamless transition to Hollywood, starring in the box-office smash hit that was

9 to 5, a spirited film with a serious message about workplace harassment. Dolly needed a spectacular gown to wear to the premiere in LA, where she'd be walking the red carpet with her co-stars, Jane Fonda and Lily Tomlin. In fact, they all turned to the film's costume designer, Ann Roth, for something fabulous. For Dolly, Roth designed a lace and satin gown complete with a faux-fur cape, both in girlish shades of pink.

Both examples would suggest that for eveningwear, Dolly favors pastels, which is an interesting way to make the color a bit spicy instead of simply sweet. Of course, a gown might not be appropriate for your average night out. But you could try a pink slip dress, with a nod to a negligee via a lace-edged hem or neckline, paired with a leather jacket—a combination that would surely get the seal of approval from Dolly.

I would then suggest defying expectations even further, by wearing a more dramatic shade during the day—just like Dolly. For her forty-second album, *Backwoods Barbie*, Robért Behar pulled out all the stops, designing a leopard-print dress with a semi-sheer coat over the top that was hot pink (and then some). What else would you wear to lounge on hay bales in the back of a pickup truck? Work the color's magic into your wardrobe with a pair of pants, a miniskirt, or even a tuxedo blazer, making sure to pare back the rest of your outfit as much as possible so that it's the pink that pops.

SCULPT YOUR SILHOUETTE

"I like to kind of show it off!"

DOLLY PARTON

*T*n almost every interview with Dolly Parton, the conversation inevitably turns not just to the way she looks, but also to her body, with some journalists enquiring after her waist size, and others even engaging in awkwardly protracted conversation involving words like "bosomy," often to delighted laughs from a studio audience. In a 1977 sit-down with Johnny Carson of *The Tonight Show*, the host said to Dolly, "I would give a year's pay to peek under there." In the same year, Barbara Walters, a veteran broadcaster at the time for ABC, asked outright: "Dolly, did you look like this when you were a kid?" "You mean the . . . full figure?" Dolly replies, laughing a little. "Yeah," says Walters. "I thought that's what you meant," Dolly says, still with a smile on her face—by now she was used to this kind of questioning. It was already a well-trodden path for a star whose appearance—and so-called assets—had become not just a conversation topic but the butt of certain jokes, many of which—Dolly being Dolly—she cracked herself.

The thing is, Dolly's favorite clothes have always fit her like a glove, hugging her in-and-out figure like nobody's business. And while of course that doesn't mean she should have to field questions about her measurements, the fact that she is often bombarded would have been enough to put some people off wearing certain things for life. But not Dolly. Even as a child, she loved feeling her clothes close to her body, crying bitterly to her mother if something she made wasn't suitably fitted. "I always wore tight clothes. When I walked down the hall, everybody was a-lookin' to see how tight my skirt was that day or how tight my sweater was. I never did like to go around half-naked but a lotta people said I might as well be naked, as tight as my clothes were. But even as a little bitty kid, if my mama made me wear somethin' that was loose on me, I used to just cry. I wanted my clothes to fit me. Even though they was rags, I wanted them to fit close to me," she said to *Rolling Stone*'s Chet Flippo.

Dolly knew exactly what she wanted and, ever-resourceful and in possession of a discerning eye, she would find ingenious ways to make her silhouette appear just so. As a youngster trying to break onto the country music scene while still at school, the fledgling singer was taken under the wing of her uncle Bill Owens. He'd ferry her to and from appearances on the radio show *The Cas Walker Farm and Home Hour*, which was based in Knoxville, and she'd borrow clothes from her Aunt Estelle, turning down the waistband of a skirt so that the hem would hit a particular spot on her thigh. And that wasn't her only attempt at DIY. She also famously took the shoulder pads out of her grandmother's coat and promptly stuck them in her bra for a bit of a boost. Even as a teenager, Dolly was already finding the silhouette that would come to be as recognizable as her high-pitched voice, which soared with vibrato—and just as unique.

Shortly after she left *The Porter Wagoner Show* in 1974, it was jumpsuits that really became Dolly's signature. Lucy Adams made her the most spectacular collection. Made of polyester, so that the singer could easily rinse them in motel room sinks when she was on the road with the band, they quite literally came in every color of the rainbow—and were embellished to the nines with trails of rhinestones up and down the extravagantly flared legs in lengths of curlicue. With long sleeves and long legs, these jumpsuits were actually quite demure, as Dolly's skin was covered from neck to wrist, waist to ankle. But what they did instead was hug in all the right places, showcasing her waist—a preference that would continue well into the next century.

In 2022, Dolly was inducted into the Rock & Roll Hall of Fame, an honor she initially refused because she didn't consider herself worthy of the title "rock star." She eventually relented and arrived onstage at the ceremony wearing an outfit that must have blown the socks off the audience, as she announced, "I'm going to have to earn it!" She wore a patent leather, or perhaps even latex, jumpsuit that had a collar to rival Elvis, with threads of gold chain adorning the hips, and chunky red crystals down the legs that matched the similarly twinkling stones on her guitar. With a keyhole cut-out at the chest, and slashes from ankle to knee that showed off her calves, it was as legendary as the stage she was singing on—and as much a testament to her style as her achievement as an artist. A year later, she produced a barnstorming rock album (*Rockstar*, 2023) that included original material, as well as covers of classics with legends such as Stevie Nicks, Debbie Harry, Emmylou Harris, and Paul McCartney.

This chapter isn't a lesson in copying Dolly's exact silhouette, although it's hard to deny its eye-catching appeal. It's more about finding shapes, among Dolly's favorites, that speak to you. Dolly emphasized certain areas and played down others—like we all do—with a dedication that meant she eventually developed a signature that she could pull out at a moment's notice. You don't need to do the same—not unless you have an appointment on the stage of the Grand Ole Opry—but it helps to know what you like and what you don't. And don't forget: A shape will never look right if it doesn't feel right on the inside.

HOW TO WEAR EXAGGERATED SILHOUETTES LIKE DOLLY'S

Just like her style, Dolly's favorite silhouettes haven't changed all that much over the years—a true sign that she knows what works for her and sticks to it religiously. As well as accentuating her waist and adding height with heels, Dolly has other tricks that she uses to create her famous shape—and, to some extent, they're all exaggerated. That doesn't mean they won't translate into your wardrobe, however. With some clever styling, they'll simply lend your look some additional flair.

FLARED PANTS

Dolly has worn flares throughout her career—from her famous bell-bottomed jumpsuits in the seventies to the frill-hemmed jeans she wore to duet with Elton John—and they're certainly not for the fainthearted, but you can still borrow a little of their "look-at-me" energy without having to go all the way. You can start with simple black pants made of wool crepe or stretch cady—both of which have a nice amount of movement in the fabric—that have a gradual flare from the waist, or more of a kick flare from the knee. (In both cases, you want the hem of your pants to just touch the floor instead of being cut off at the ankle.) Although you might initially feel like you're cosplaying a seventies rock star, flares will add length to your legs, especially if you wear them with decent heels, and they will look sharper than a straight-up-and-down silhouette. The golden rule is to always tuck in your top half, because a hem that hits the upper thigh will immediately shorten your legs. Once you've got a feel for big-energy flares, you can play around with different colors. How about a cherry red flare with a butter yellow turtleneck? Or lavender with chocolate? Or hot pink with navy blue? Seriously, once you get the hang of wearing flares, you'll wonder how you ever lived without them.

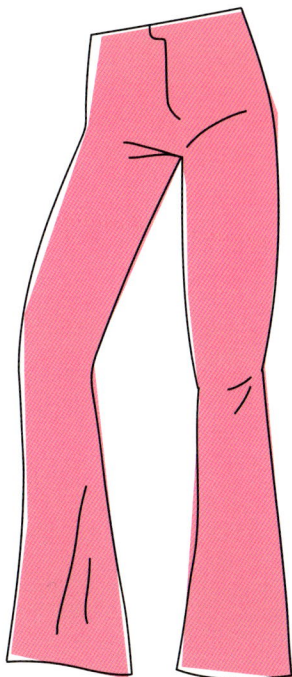

CAPRI PANTS

Dolly has often been seen sporting a pair of denim capri pants, a pants style otherwise known as "pedal pushers" that was popular in the late nineties and early aughties, with a high waist, a close fit, and a cropped length that can finish anywhere from just under the knee to an inch or two above the mid-calf. (Dolly wears them all the time to perform and, as you'd expect, hers are usually embellished.) Although that might sound very short for pants, they're a seriously chic proposition in black, especially when styled with a slingback kitten heel, a leather clog, or a mule sandal (Dolly's absolute favorite). Because it's such a specific kind of shape—creating a streamlined effect down the body—it's wise to go simple elsewhere, with something like a cropped sweater or a checked blazer to keep everything nicely in balance.

XL SLEEVES

Dolly's stage routines often involved switching between different instruments, which meant she didn't do a whole lot of dancing. What she did do, however, was lift her arms up to the heavens, which was the perfect opportunity to show off the batwing sleeves of her dresses or jumpsuits. You can so easily bring a sense of drama to what you're wearing, as well as drawing attention to your waist thanks to the contrast, by choosing the right sleeve—something that demands to be noticed, whether it's a puff at the shoulder or a trumpet at the wrist. As part of the artwork for *Backwoods Barbie*, Dolly wore a gingham blouse with girlishly puffed sleeves. It's a style that you see summer in, summer out, especially in airy white cotton—and for good reason. It does all the hard work for you, pairing with anything from cargo pants to a button-front linen skirt.

SHARP SHOULDERS

Whenever Dolly wears jackets, they're cut to certain proportions, standing out at the shoulders and hugging the waist. And it's a silhouette that works brilliantly for most bust sizes, especially if the jacket's cropped to just above the hip. But why does it have to have a big shoulder, you might ask. As Dolly could tell you, an exaggerated shoulder helps to create more of an hourglass silhouette. The word "exaggerated" might bring back memories of shoulder pads, but really, it's much less extreme than the power look of the eighties. You're simply looking for a little sharpness, which a lot of blazers already have built into their shoulders. That way, you can wear your blazer with baggy jeans and still look put together.

CREATING A WAIST

As discussed, Dolly's waistline has been the source of much speculation over the years, especially by interviewers who seemed to think it their journalistic duty to use colorful language to describe her figure. But purely from a style perspective, it is undeniable that her waist is an area she has always liked to accentuate. So how can you create a similar effect, especially if you don't feel you have much of a waist in the first place?

For straight-up-and-down figures, it's trickier, as you're essentially trying to create instead of accentuate. It's not impossible, though; it simply involves tricking the eye, guiding it toward certain points to give the impression of a waist like Dolly's.

Take the simplest combination in the book:
a pair of jeans and a T-shirt. If your jeans are
straight and your tee is untucked, your waist
is going to get completely lost. But if your
jeans are flared and you tuck your tee *in*, then
you're drawing the eye in (at the waist) then out
(at the ankle). Why not include another favorite
item of Dolly's—the sharp-shouldered blazer?
Add one of those into the equation and you're really
creating that in-and-out silhouette associated with
an hourglass.

If you want to draw attention to your waist, a
strategically positioned belt is the solution. I prefer
a middle-of-the-road width as opposed to thick
or thin, though, as it stands out while being only
a subtle intrusion into whatever you're
cinching—a trench coat, a sweaterdress, or
similar. And for an even faster way to draw the
eye to your waist, simply wear a crop top with
high-waisted pants that fit like a glove
around your stomach, so that just a sliver of
skin is on show. Dolly's age-old trick is to
tie your shirt at the waist, as shown on the
cover of 1977's *Here You Come Again*. Just
like the song, this look doesn't get old.

WHY YOU SHOULD JUMP INTO

A jumpsuit is a ready-made outfit so, really, nothing could be easier to wear—right? Yes and no. Dolly certainly relied on them a lot in the seventies, travelling with a special repair kit so that she could replace any lost rhinestones from the comfort of the tour bus. But Dolly's were tailor-made by Lucy Adams, which means they fitted her body to perfection. That's the thing about buying a jumpsuit—it can be hard to find one that's a ten out of ten in terms of fit, because, obviously, we're all bringing different torsos and legs to the table, as well as different dress sizes. Once you have found the one, however, it will become such a hardworking piece in your wardrobe that you almost certainly won't begrudge the legwork you put in to get there, I promise! It's also worth noting that you might have to get your jumpsuit tailored in order to achieve the same glove-like fit as Dolly's, which will 100 percent be worth it.

So, where do you start? I strongly recommend going to a department store so that you can try on jumpsuits from lots of different brands at once, doing yourself an immediate favor by saving time on endless online returns. Take a bunch of sizes into the changing room and pay attention to how each fits your waist, your legs, and your bottom. Hopefully, you'll leave with something that will make those mornings when nothing seems to go together just a little bit easier.

But before you walk off into the sunset with your new jumpsuit, we're not quite done. As well as thinking about the fit, you've also got to consider the style. There are so many different "personalities" when it comes to jumpsuits. You've got coveralls—a utilitarian style made of cotton with a loose silhouette that's ideal for off-duty. "Evening" jumpsuits is a broader category, which covers every kind of dressier all-in-one—from halter-neck to embellished— and these are almost guaranteed to have a fitted waist and a more fluid material. Then you've got overalls. And if you think you're too old to be considering the same overalls you wore as a kid, Dolly wore a much-beloved pair on the cover of *Hungry Again*—and she was fifty-two. In addition to denim, you can buy dungarees in tactile fabrics like corduroy and velvet, which can make the whole look a degree more luxurious, especially if you wear something like a cashmere sweater or a crushed silk shirt underneath.

JUMPSUITS

EMBELLISH TO THE NINES

"A rhinestone
shines just as good
as a diamond."

DOLLY PARTON

Dolly Parton is someone who shines, quite literally, in rhinestone-encrusted regalia, but her first brush with something you could consider embellishment was much more down-to-earth. As a young girl playing in the great outdoors with her siblings, she found bird feathers in the forest that she'd stick in her hair as a rudimentary kind of adornment, as well as wearing "necklaces" made from string and acorns. Even as a child she wanted to look her best, a mantra she carried with her when she moved out of her hometown. She was in such a hurry to get to the home of country music and become a star, she headed to Nashville the day after she graduated.

In Nashville, the stars looked a certain way, with outfits weighed down by spangles and hair like Cool Whip. It was this specific blueprint for glamour—wholesome yet womanly—that became like Dolly's bread and butter, the fledgling songwriter and singer who went hawking her musical wares around the city, hoping to catch the eye (or perhaps that should be ear?) of Nashville's established talents, before she got her break on *The Porter Wagoner Show*. Wagoner had a very distinctive look himself, with his own signature hairdo and flashy suits, and Dolly quickly started to shine just as brightly thanks to her designers at the time, Ruth Kemp and Lucy Adams, who, by all accounts, were thrilled that their client wanted her attire to be turbocharged with twinkle. Some of Dolly's outfits took several days to make because they were so heavily embellished, and, at one point, Lucy was ordering three hundred dollars' worth of rhinestones a week because the demand for dazzle was so high.

In 1974, when Dolly eventually left the show to spread her wings, her outfits became even more embellished—and not just with rhinestones, but also with sequins, feathers, beads, fringe, buttons, and pearls—anything that added an extra something.

For a 1978 episode of *Cher*, Dolly wore a stupendous gown by Bob Mackie, the iconic designer who made clothes for every star in the constellation: Marilyn Monroe, Tina Turner, Barbra Streisand, and, of course, Cher. Dolly's dress was sequinned and black, with a spray of feathers at the sleeves and at the hem, and it also had a trail of emerald-colored crystals that gave it a glint. From there, the sky was the limit when it came to extravagant costumes (and embellishment).

During the eighties, Dolly became a household name in Hollywood—she was now a bona fide movie star as well as being a massive musical success, and her outfits were suitably high octane (both on-screen and off). In the 1984 film *Rhinestone*, she outshone her co-star Sylvester Stallone—not only because he wasn't a trained singer, but because, as you can infer from the movie's title, Dolly's character also wore *a lot* of rhinestones. Designed by Theadora Van Runkle, who also created Dolly's costumes in *The Best*

Little Whorehouse in Texas, one dress had a fringed skirt that was made up of strands of rhinestones that ran from waist to ankle. But it was Tony Chase who truly made Dolly glow as she'd never glowed before. The two started working together for ABC's *Dolly*—the singer's variety show that ran for two years from 1987— and it was a relationship that bore fruit of the fabulous variety. The dress that sums it up best is the one that Dolly wore on the album cover for *White Limozeen* (1989). She'd arrived—and this dress, weighty with spangles, yet somehow like a second skin on Dolly, was unforgettable.

TONY CHASE

Dolly certainly found a kindred spirit in Tony Chase. The New York–born designer was the man responsible for ushering her wardrobe into its most glamorous era. As Dolly became a hot property in Hollywood, Tony was by her side, creating some truly iconic looks for career milestones like the 1989 cover of *White Limozeen*. Dolly was also transformed into an angel by his sleight of hand for that same year's CMA Awards, which was entirely appropriate, as she was singing "He's Alive," one of her spiritual songs. The sleeves of the dress were winged and sewn with white beads so that it looked almost like Dolly could take flight as she raised her arms to the heavens. Tony's showmanship was also put to good use on a famous shoot for *Vanity Fair* in 1991. Dolly was lifted onto the shoulders of servicemen in the US Air Force, her spangled halter-neck gown and shoulder-grazing star earrings contrasting with the sea of camouflaged personnel around her. It must have been a pinch-me moment to behold, and the look was a favorite of Tony's, who passed away just a few years later in 1994.

A WORD ON BUTTERFLIES

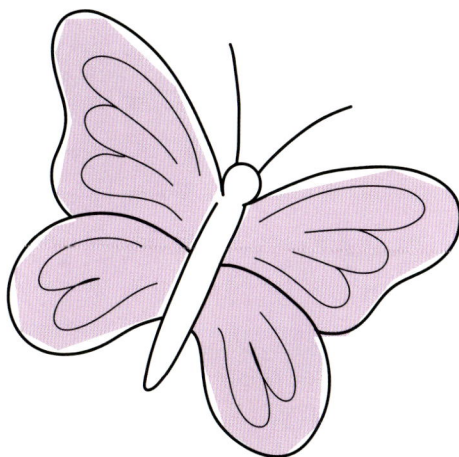

The butterfly has long been associated with Dolly. There's her song, "Love Is Like a Butterfly" (1974), a track of an album of the same name that has a magnificent pair of multicolored wings on the cover, and then there's also the fact that she's often been called an "iron butterfly," due to her steely business acumen that is somewhat hidden beneath a soft exterior of blonde hair and billowing chiffon. In a more literal sense, the insect's outline also featured on a lot of Dolly's costumes, picked out in rhinestones or even buttons so that it "flew" across whatever she was wearing. Interestingly, the butterfly is now associated with Y2K, an aesthetic made famous by pop stars like Mariah Carey, Britney Spears, and Dua Lipa, who have all incorporated the butterfly's image into their wardrobes. But we know the truth—Dolly got there first.

HOW TO WEAR EMBELLISHMENT IN EVERYDAY LIFE

It's hard to make a swirl of rhinestones or a plume of feathers look casual enough for everyday wear, but if you asked Dolly, she would say that it's more than OK to bring a touch of theatricality to your 9-to-5. In fact, working a little embellishment into your wardrobe can be surprisingly wearable when done right.

FEATHERED PAJAMAS

A feathered pair of silky pajama bottoms are louche, comfortable, and surprisingly low effort for something that looks so special. Pajamas . . . outside the bedroom? I haven't lost the plot! It's just that lots of brands are now making pajama-style pants that have feathery hems. Some even come with button-down pajama tops with similarly feathered sleeves. And while their vibe is distinctly Old Hollywood, they're also very easy to wear if you dress them down—a gray crewneck sweater, a leather jacket, and a pair of silver kitten heels are all you need to bring something a little extra to your average day at work. (FYI, although black is not a color that Dolly wears very much, I do think it's the best color to choose if you're putting on feathered pajama bottoms for a regular day. A macaron-sweet pastel pair could, perhaps, be a step too far into the realm of "boudoir" for public transport.)

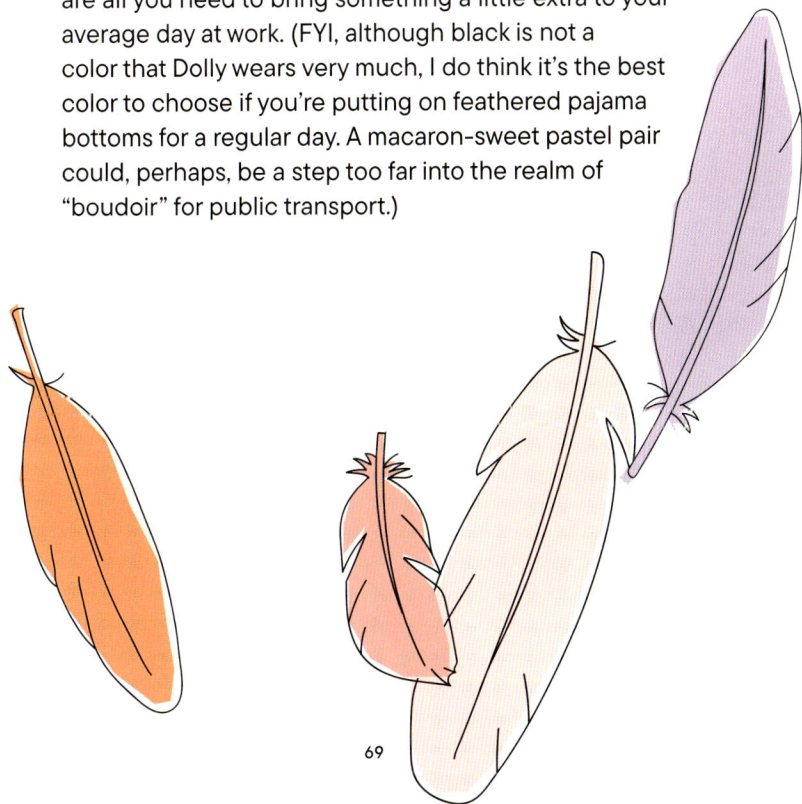

BUTTONED SKIRTS

Customization can be a risky business, but most people have the basic needle skills required to change a button. Dolly might have preferred rhinestones, but the humble button was still used to brilliant effect on some of the two-piece outfits made for her by Lucy Adams, who used a bunch of different colors to pep up white tailoring. Changing up the buttons on, say, a simple denim maxi skirt will instantly give it a point of interest (or several, in fact). All you have to do is carefully snip off the old buttons so that you can take them with you to a haberdashery—or measure them if you're buying your buttons online—so that you've got the right diameter at hand. You could also try the same trick on a jacket, which will allow for bigger and more elaborate button options.

PEARL JACKETS

A lot of Dolly's most extravagant dresses also had a
smattering of pearls in among the rhinestones, as
was the case with the spectacular gown she wore for
one of the premieres of the classic film *Steel Magnolias*,
which had a delicate network of "icicles" on the sleeves,
each one shaking with tiny seed pearls. The good news
is that pearls are now everywhere you look—and not
just on ears. A lot of brands are now using pearls as a
rather modern embellishment on the collars of sweaters
and denim jackets, as well as on the pockets of jeans.

RICKRACK JEANS

While on the subject of jeans, you can now buy many different varieties, including those that have been elevated with embellishments such as rhinestones and rickrack (the wiggly add-on that will probably remind you of a childhood art project). Dolly's early stage costumes were often edged with a patterned strip that reminded her of rickrack—an enhancement that she remembers fondly from her own childhood, when her mother would use it to decorate the dresses she made out of flour sacks. If you've got patience and a steady hand, you could easily use rickrack to decorate the hem of your favorite jeans, giving them a bit of country flavor that would look retro yet cute with a crewneck sweater in the same hue.

CRYSTAL HEELS

Dolly wears crystals like they're going out of fashion, which, of course, they aren't. So much so that you can now buy shoes that are suitably frosted, whether it's a crystal buckle, an ankle strap, a studded heel, or an allover smattering that means everywhere but the sole is positively sparkling. Whichever iteration you choose, it's such an easy way to look instantly more polished, especially if you're wearing something low-key, like cargo pants.

DAZZLE
IN
DENIM

"I think denim's always going to be associated with country music."

DOLLY PARTON

Even though the glitz has become part and parcel of what makes Dolly Parton, Dolly Parton, you get the sense that she's just as at home wearing denim as she is wearing something bedazzled.

When she decided to try bluegrass, releasing a trio of albums in the late nineties and early aughts that constituted a kind of homecoming for the star, who was returning to the soulful music of the mountains, denim seemed like the natural choice. It was her way of signaling to her fans that she was rediscovering her roots. For 2002's *Halos & Horns*, which was the third in the series and photographed by Annie Leibovitz, she wore a denim shirt that she'd had in her wardrobe for three decades.

It's a fabric that obviously feels as familiar as an old friend to Dolly, who's made it her own over the years with help from her designer partners in crime. It's also a fabric that goes hand in hand with traditional country stars. Loretta Lynn famously wore denim pantsuits with contrast stitching throughout her career. Dolly, meanwhile, did her own take on the country signature with a denim two-piece suit designed by Tony Chase, which had roses blooming on either hip.

No matter the occasion, Dolly puts her own stamp on denim, usually wearing her jeans with—what else?—a heel, another signature that she's rarely seen without. In 1977, she released her nineteenth album, *Here You Come Again*. Despite facing some criticism from her country fan base, it was the singer's most serious attempt to cross over to a pop audience. And it worked. The album sold a million copies, and on its cover was a surprisingly dressed-down Dolly, wearing jeans and a stacked heel that saved the denim from looking in any way dull. It's a duo that she brought out again and again, always wearing denim her own way, and one that you, too, can easily work into your wardrobe.

DOLLY'S DENIM THROUGH THE AGES

NEW HARVEST . . . FIRST GATHERING – 1977

For the cover of *New Harvest . . . First Gathering*, Dolly sat in the passenger seat of a car, wearing a denim jacket with a paisley scarf tied around her hair, a look that was as wholesome as the country sound of the album.

HERE YOU COME AGAIN – 1977

Dolly wore one of her simplest outfits on the cover of *Here You Come Again*, but it's also one of her most effective. The only concessions to what was fast becoming her signature brand of glamour were her hair and her heels.

HUNGRY AGAIN
– 1998

After "arriving" in Hollywood, with smash-hit films under her belt such as *9 to 5*, *The Best Little Whorehouse in Texas,* and *Steel Magnolias*, the nineties signaled a period of reflection for Dolly, which you could quite clearly see on the cover of *Hungry Again*. She's sitting on a wooden swing seat, wearing denim overalls, with her hair tied in a braid over one shoulder. It was raw—a world away from the shine and shimmer of the eighties.

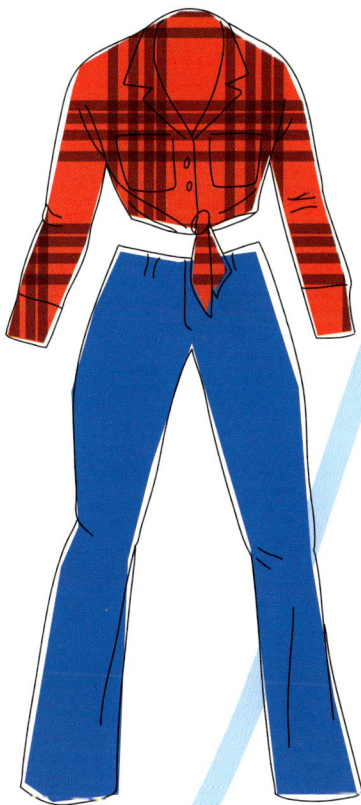

RUN, ROSE, RUN – 2022

For *Run, Rose, Run*, the album that shared the name of her bestselling novel written with James Patterson, Dolly proved that if it ain't broke, don't fix it by wearing a plaid shirt and denim flares in an ensemble that was pure country. The singer summed up her relationship with the age-old fabric on Instagram, saying, "Denim's always a do."

DRESSED-UP DENIM

The majority of us probably pull on a pair of jeans most days of the week. They're almost like a second skin—a day-in, day-out garment that doesn't require much thought because they go with everything. But that's not the case for Dolly. It's true that the singer does wear dressed-down denim, as discussed earlier, but she also wears the opposite: dressed-*up* denim. And I mean up.

In 2005, Dolly wore an exuberant denim outfit to perform with Elton John. In an interview with *Vogue*, as part of its video series "Life in Looks," she joked that she looked like Little Lord Fauntleroy. The outfit in question was a lace tailcoat complete with gold frogging, as well as a pair of jeans that were sequinned down the legs and frilled at the hems. "Of course, I was trying to dress like Elton John. And he was trying to look like someone else during that time, I guess. He was dressing down. And I was dressing up!"

On a red carpet in 2006, Dolly arrived wearing a cropped denim bolero jacket that was bedazzled with a smattering of crystals, silvery beads, and stars. On her bottom half, she wore denim capri pants, similarly embellished, as well as a rhinestone belt made up of interlinked hearts that hugged her hips.

While rhinestones are definitely one way to do dressed-up denim, with several brands now making jeans whose legs come dotted with crystals to give the everyday an extra twinkle, you can also look for slightly more subtle nods to embellishment. You can also get jeans that are logoed, printed, coated with metallics, or panelled with leather— each of which is a fabulous way to make the ordinary a little more extraordinary.

If you want to dress up your denim but still want to be able to wear it all the time, try patchworking. As well as being an excellent way to use up scraps of old denim, it also means that your new jeans will be a one-off. Just like Dolly Parton.

DOUBLE

Before double denim gained a reputation as being a one-way ticket to tackiness in the aughts, all the rock stars (Elvis Presley), pop stars (Cher), and country stars (Tammy Wynette) were wearing it. Dolly's music might defy categorization, but she, too, was a fan of denim on denim (in fact, she even dared to do triple denim sometimes, by also adding a pair of true-blue cowboy boots into the equation). In a rare off-duty photo, she appeared in a pair of snatch-waisted jeans and a matching jacket that might have been a nod to her famous "coat of many colors" with its green collar, yellow pockets, and red cuffs. It was very eighties—more country glam than casual—but is still a blueprint for how to wear the look today.

As sensational as it looked on Dolly, a slightly easier fit for your head-to-toe denim will probably be more forgiving, and I personally tend to take a relaxed approach when wearing head-to-toe denim.

DENIM

DOUBLE

It's a uniform that you can pull on when you don't want to think about what you're wearing, when you want to blend into the background, but still look put together. Instead of matching my top half to my bottom half—with two denims that are exactly the same blue—it's easier to take mismatched hues and create more of a patchwork effect. I have a light-wash denim maxi skirt that looks great with a darker-indigo jacket. Black or ecru jeans will go with almost any shade of denim if you want to make things easier. You could also tuck a pocketed denim shirt into a straight midi skirt, finishing the look with a pair of scrunched knee boots. Alternatively, leave the shirt untucked for a slouchier vibe that isn't quite so seventies.

Follow Dolly's lead when it comes to what to wear with your double denim: a basic white tee. Add a low-maintenance shoe like a loafer and you're good to go. It's really that simple.

DENIM

HOW TO FIND A PAIR OF JEANS THAT ACTUALLY FITS

Dolly's jeans fit like they were tailor-made, but is it actually possible to buy a pair that's perfect? From my experience in the field, I would say it's rare. They're usually too tight, too loose, too short, too long, or cleave nicely to your tummy while cutting off the blood supply to your bottom half. (That's my experience at least, as someone who's a "triangle" with a smaller waist and bigger hips.) Unfortunately, there's no shortcut. Buying a pair of jeans that hugs you in all the right places is simply a case of trial and error. But persevere and, eventually, you'll find "the one." In the meantime, here are some rules to live by:

★ **Always try jeans on.** Dolly once admitted that she doesn't buy clothes off the rack because of her unique proportions. This is a good lesson when you're buying jeans, because they're one of the hardest garments to get right. Unless you've bought the exact same pair of jeans before, it isn't a good idea to shop online. Since there's essentially no standardization at all across brands meaning a size 12 could be wildly different from one brand to the next—you need to take lots of different sizes into the fitting room and try, try, try.

★ **Look for brands who offer different leg lengths.** It's very annoying when you buy a pair of jeans that's a few inches too long or short. Luckily, more chain store brands are starting to offer different leg lengths that are tailored to a variety of heights.

★ **Use online tools to find your size.** A lot of shops now have gauges that tell you whether a garment comes up small, big, or fits "true to size," as well as online fit calculators, which ask for information such as height, weight, and inside leg measurement before calculating the size that should fit you the best.

★ **Take your jeans to a tailor.** Dolly may very well get her jeans tailored so that they really fit her figure to perfection. This is a great option if you want to avoid buying stretch denim, which is less sustainable than pure cotton, due to its blended fabrication that takes longer to break down. Your local dry cleaner will be able to take in a waist or turn up a hem quite easily.

★ **Don't wash your jeans too often.** Because machine-washing tends to shrink jeans, overwashing can result in a shrink-stretch cycle that can leave your denim looking a little worse for wear. If need be, spot clean or steam before resorting to chucking them in the machine. And please— never, ever tumble dry your jeans.

SHINE
IN
METALLICS

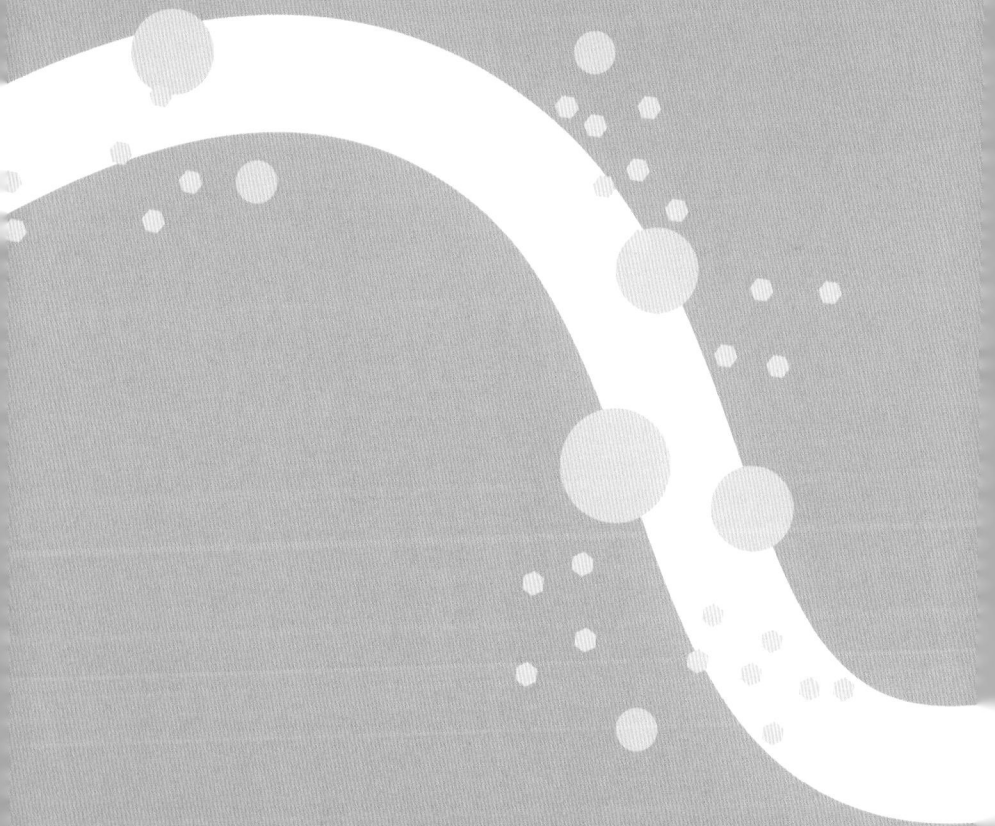

"I want to be somebody that extremely shines."

DOLLY PARTON

*T*n her seminal 1978 sit-down with *Playboy*'s Lawrence Grobel, an interview which caused some of her more conservative fans to raise a collective eyebrow because of the magazine's "colorful" editorials, Dolly stated, point-blank, that she wanted to be famous. It's something she had been saying since her high school graduation ceremony, when each child had to tell the audience what they hoped to achieve once they'd graduated. In her eyes, a star was someone who positively emanated light—exactly like the kind of star you see in the sky. "A star shines, of course, but I want to be really radiant," she said to Grobel. That was the final word of the interview. And despite the fact that she wasn't talking about her clothes at that particular moment, you can't help but think that "radiant" is a rather apt descriptor for a wardrobe that is quite literally designed to dazzle an audience.

In fact, Dolly often wears the set of colors that have come to be associated with stars: metallics. At 2022's ACM Awards, held in Las Vegas, she was transformed into a walking disco ball thanks to Steve Summers, her creative director since 2004. Wearing a bodysuit that was given a surface of mirrorlike shards, making every inch of her five-foot-one-inch frame shine, it was almost a literal interpretation of what she said forty-four years ago. She really was radiant.

You don't have to aim for the same mega-wattage as Dolly, but introduce metallics into your wardrobe and, believe me, you'll sense an increase in your own star power. Because who doesn't want to shine a little in life?

HOW TO WEAR METALLICS IN YOUR EVERYDAY WARDROBE

Dolly Parton doesn't tend to do things by halves, so when she wears metallics, it's often a head-to-toe affair. Sometimes, though, she only wears a glint, and it's this relaxed approach that you can work into your wardrobe. Performing in Phoenix, Arizona, as part of 2014's Blue Smoke World Tour, Dolly wore a gold vest over a billowing white shirt. And because the rest of her outfit was relatively pared back, the eye was immediately drawn straight to her glimmering torso.

One of the easiest ways to find a similar kind of "statement" metallic that you can incorporate into an otherwise everyday outfit is silver leather. Whether it's a straight-legged pair of pants or a single-breasted blazer that's cut on the oversized side, the material has a matte surface, which means that it doesn't shimmer while still also making a statement (albeit a more subtle one). Brands nowadays have so many brilliant iterations of silver leather pants—some of which are actually coated denim as opposed to calfskin—as well as blazers, which should have minimal bells and whistles because too many details can easily take a jacket into fussy territory.

SILVER LEATHER PANTS

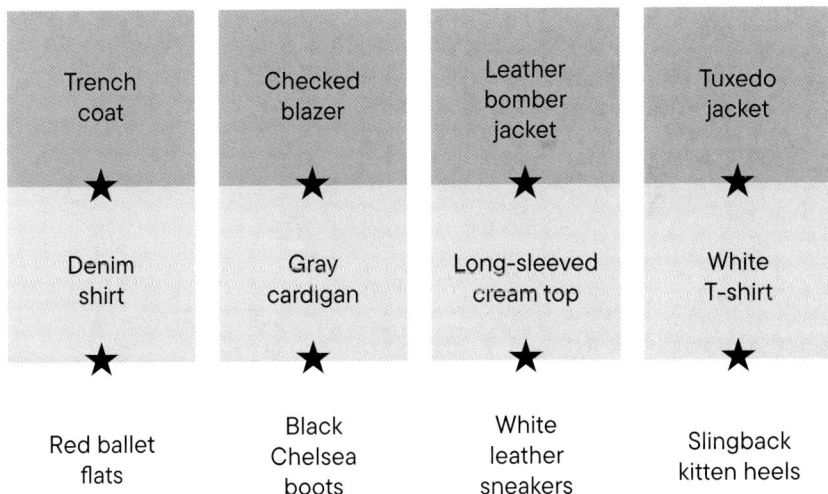

Trench coat	Checked blazer	Leather bomber jacket	Tuxedo jacket
★	★	★	★
Denim shirt	Gray cardigan	Long-sleeved cream top	White T-shirt
★	★	★	★
Red ballet flats	Black Chelsea boots	White leather sneakers	Slingback kitten heels

The other way to wear metallics is via your accessories. Dolly's shoe collection includes towering gold mules, as well as thigh-high silver boots that are wrapped with buckles from ankle to knee like intergalactic stage armor. A more wearable version might be silver ankle boots with a pointed toe to elongate your leg. And because silver is almost a neutral, in that it goes with almost every shade from the vanilla to the more va-va-voom, you can treat them like they're a black pair of boots, using them to add some metallic flair to a pantsuit, a denim skirt, or a sweaterdress. I also rate gold ballet flats highly, which are brilliant at making a "boring" outfit of, say, a shirt and jeans look, well, less boring and more intentional. The same effect can be achieved with a smart metallic shoulder bag that sits snugly under the armpit, which has the miraculous effect of making everything near it look sharper.

GOLD BALLET FLATS

Trench coat	Checked blazer	Camel cocoon coat	Leather blouson
★	★	★	★
White shirt	Denim jumpsuit	White T-shirt	Black crewneck sweater
★	★	★	★
Straight-legged jeans	Silver hoop earrings	Burgundy wool skirt	Black miniskirt

HOW TO WEAR SILVER AND GOLD TOGETHER

The fun starts when you mix your metallics. First of all, banish the notion that you should only wear silver *or* gold, along with the idea that the two should never meet. It's one of those unspoken fashion rules that doesn't make any sense at all—just like the "rule" that navy doesn't go with black, or pink with red. Those combinations don't only work, they also convey a sense of power and confidence. They're also fun. Dolly is a connoisseur of not following the rules, of course, and has worn some very memorable outfits that absolutely throw caution to the wind when it comes to cocktails of colors.

In one of her most famous roles—as Miss Mona, the sexpot madam in *The Best Little Whorehouse in Texas*—Dolly was in her element (she compared the character to actress Mae West, one of her all-time icons).

Unfortunately, the production itself was beset by difficulties, many of which involved its leading man, Burt Reynolds, but the clothes positively sizzled on-screen. In one scene, Miss Mona wears a metallic lamé dress that is half silver, half gold, with a fault line down the middle that made it a match in metallic heaven. It was quite something to behold, as the gown's hemline was sewn onto bracelets that were worn at the wrist, so the dress showed a hint of calf, as well as shoulders and cleavage.

It might be difficult to replicate such an article of clothing, but you can start by mixing your metals. I used to be a real stickler for only wearing gold or silver jewelry, even checking the snap closures on my jeans and the zipper on my jacket because it would bother me if everything wasn't coordinated. Thankfully, I've seen the light, and I now wear silver hoops next to their gold cousins. I even have rings that come in a set of one silver, one gold. That's how well the two go together. You don't need to buy anything new, of course, but if you're in the market, keep your eye out for pieces that actually combine the two metals, like earrings that have chunky threads of both, creating a hoop that will make you look twice.

If you want to go a step further, you can try wearing, for example, a simply cut silver leather jacket with gold kitten heels.

You just need to make sure that the rest of your outfit is as minimal as possible. A "white tank top and indigo jeans" kind of minimal. That way, your metallics will be the moment.

WEAR "MORE IS MORE" HAIR AND MAKEUP

"I always liked to wear a lot of makeup, more than probably I should wear. But I think more is more and whoever made up that 'less is more' is full of it."

DOLLY PARTON

*T*n the unlikely event that you've never heard any music by Dolly Parton (she's won 12 Grammys and released 66 albums, and written an estimated 3,000 songs, FYI)—you probably still have a fairly accurate idea of what she looks like. It's a look that hasn't really changed since she emerged onto the country scene as a teenager in the late fifties, singing on a radio broadcast by Cas Walker, a businessman, politician, and general mover and shaker in Knoxville, Tennessee. Dolly Parton's younger sister Stella remembers her older sibling's mania for hair at the time. In Stephen Miller's biography of the singer, *Smart Blonde*, Stella says that Dolly's hair had to be high and big; the trend for "teasing" (backcombing the roots of your hair to create va-va-voom volume) was all the rage at the time. "It was a showgirl hairdo."

Even before she started performing or cultivating a look that would eventually become an almost patented part of "brand Dolly," the

WEAR "MORE IS MORE" HAIR AND MAKEUP

singer had an early fascination with makeup as
a child. Owing to her circumstances, however,
she had to be resourceful in order to get her fix.
She often tells the story of how she foraged her
very first makeup kit in the mountains where
she was born, fashioning lip stain out of a
chemical called Merthiolate, face powder out of
flour, and an eyebrow pencil out of singed
matches. She didn't give a hoot about what her
father thought about her makeshift makeup.
As she once told *Playboy*: "I'd paint my lips and
there was nothin' Daddy could do. He couldn't
rub it off. He would say, 'Get that lipstick off
you!' And I'd say, 'It won't come off, it's my
natural coloring, Daddy.' Then he'd say, 'Bull.'"
With the benefit of hindsight, it seems obvious
that her childhood rebellion was an early sign
of what was to come, and how makeup would
always be something she took immense
pleasure in. In the years that followed, she
refused to tone down her look for anyone,
despite their best efforts, and she even sang
a song about false eyelashes on her second

album, *Just Because I'm a Woman*. Dolly went on to make a metallic lid, a flushed cheek, and a glossy lip as much a part of her image as her wigs (which she's worn religiously since the sixties, because all the backcombing eventually started to damage her natural hair).

Dolly has told humorous anecdotes over the years about how she's always fully made-up at home in case there's an emergency, which seems to be corroborated by one of her most famous co-stars and friends, Jane Fonda. When they were working together on the movie *9 to 5*, the three lead actors—Lily Tomlin, Jane Fonda, and Dolly herself—would throw pajama parties to get to know each other. But in an interview as part of the 2019 documentary *Dolly Parton: Here I Am*, Fonda recalls that even during these sleepovers, where you assume you'd see someone at their most natural, she "never saw [Dolly] without her regalia." In fact, the film's famous title song, also called "9 to 5," wouldn't have happened without a very important part of Dolly: her fake nails. She was wandering around the set one day when she just started "playing" her acrylics, tapping out that oh-so-catchy beat that mimics the sound of a typewriter starting off the song.

Just as the movie *9 to 5* wouldn't be the same without that song, Dolly wouldn't be the same without her makeup. This is how to copy her "more is more" approach, while still making it true to you.

EYES

Dolly might have been a country singer, but in the late seventies her eye makeup was pure disco, a metallic explosion from her upper lash line to the arch of her eyebrow. As well as often matching her shadow's pigment to her outfit, she wasn't afraid of experimenting. And that's the whole point. A frosted eyelid might sound intimidatingly bold, but it's just about playing—and perhaps even ripping up the rule book that tells you to stick to a smoky eye or nothing.

You probably already have a good idea about what colors suit you depending on the shade of your pupils and brows, but if you're looking for inspiration, Parton often favored a rosy pink lid. It's a color that people sometimes avoid because it's more associated with cheeks than eyes, but why not use it for both? Paired with fanned-out lashes—which have either been teased with a mascara wand and an eyelash curler or enhanced with individual false lashes that you can easily buy at beauty stores—it flushes your face with a warmth, a dewiness, that has a "hard country" kind of wholesomeness. And for another idea, why not try a misty white lid with a carefully applied swoop of liquid eyeliner that curls ever so slightly upward at the outer corner of the eye? It's a look that's lifted straight off the back cover of 1977's *New Harvest . . . First Gathering*, and it has retro appeal while still looking strikingly modern thanks to its monochrome palette.

NAILS

For someone who often has to strum a guitar onstage, Parton has impressively long nails—squared at the ends and extending almost an inch above the tip of each finger. Although the shape and length have varied over the years, she has mostly always stuck to red for the color—that primary, full-bodied, lipstick shade of red that somehow manages to make whatever you're wearing look more intentional, more polished. Perhaps this preference for always having painted nails was inevitable. Dolly's "mountain" makeup kit also included pokeberries, a round, black berry that grows on a deep pink stem, which she'd use to give herself a rudimentary manicure as a little girl.

If you've never tried false nails, I would recommend strengthening yours beforehand with one of the many treatments you can buy from any good nail brand. And for first-timers, you don't have to opt for an inch-long acrylic. That might be one to work up to once you've gotten used to how false nails feel on your fingers. An almond-shaped nail whose point extends about half a centimeter above the tip of your actual nail might be a better way to ease yourself in. Having said that, Dolly can play the banjo while wearing hers (although she did have to sit out the volleyball games played by her bandmates while they were on the road). So, what are you waiting for?

LIPS

Dolly's endearingly wide smile—readily bestowed and often captured—means that your eye is often drawn to her mouth first. In one of the outrageously fun photographs of the pint-sized singer with Arnold Schwarzenegger, which were taken in 1977 by Annie Leibovitz, Dolly stands with her hands on her hips—her wig obscuring the face of the cartoonishly muscly specimen who's flexing his biceps in the background—part smiling, part laughing. The photoshoot was part of an interview in *Rolling Stone*—Schwarzenegger was simply a prop that occasionally (and no doubt obligingly) picked up his co-star—and her lips are indeed the first thing you're drawn to, despite the wig, the rhinestone jumpsuit, and the two sets of thighs on show. They're colored pink, almost exactly the same hue as her spangled jumpsuit by Lucy Adams, and look beguilingly shiny. That's because she swears by lip gloss, which sometimes gets a bad rap, but is one of the best tools in your makeup bag. Whether you apply it straight onto your lips or use it to give a matte lipstick some extra shine, it somehow looks sumptuous.

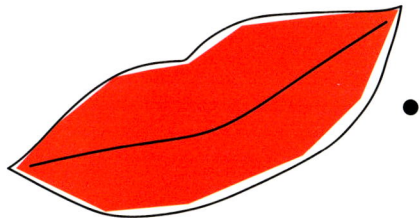

HAIR

Dolly's first big hit was a song called "Dumb Blonde" (1967), which is perhaps why her luminous (and loftily styled) hair became such an important part of her brand. And whether it was teased into a platinum bouffant in the sixties or fluffed into something altogether more poodle-like in the eighties, Dolly's gravity-defying hairstyles are mostly thanks to an impressive array of wigs. Whenever she's asked how many she owns, the singer usually quips that she has one for every day of the year (although the actual number could be significantly higher, considering that she sometimes wore not just one, but three at a time). Not only did her wigs add crucial height—and spare her real hair from a lifetime of backcombing—but they're rather like her personality: larger-than-life (and unapologetically so).

Perhaps you're toying with the idea of getting a wig, in which case take a look at the following pages for inspiration on just how big it's safe to go (hint: very). Or maybe you're simply weighing up whether or not to go for something a little more extroverted in the hair department. Either way, remember that Dolly once wore a wig that had tiny bows tied into its elaborate curls in the seventies—the definition of big-energy hair.

DOLLY'S WONDERFUL WIGS

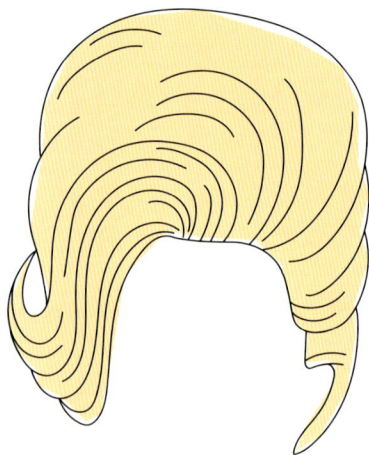

1965

Dolly's sixties wigs were backcombed up and away from her head into a full beehive, while the ends curled into a ski jump-style flick around the side of her face.

1970

In her jumpsuit era, Dolly favored a wig that was backcombed at the crown so that it added a good half a foot to her height. Curled around her face into large ringlets, it was as over-the-top (quite literally) as its wearer.

1979

Toward the end of the decade, her wig was a true platinum shade. Rounded and curled, it paired brilliantly with, say, an elaborately ruffled dress.

1989

A decade later, Dolly's hair embraced the eighties, with a permed wig that came with fully grown bangs and a cascade of tight curls that flowed down her back.

1993

In the nineties, Dolly preferred wigs that were straighter and fluffier, fanning inward at her shoulders.

2014

Dolly's wigs might have been smaller in size in the last decade—feathery and light around her face—but they still made a statement, albeit a more subtle one.

PLAY
WITH
LEATHER

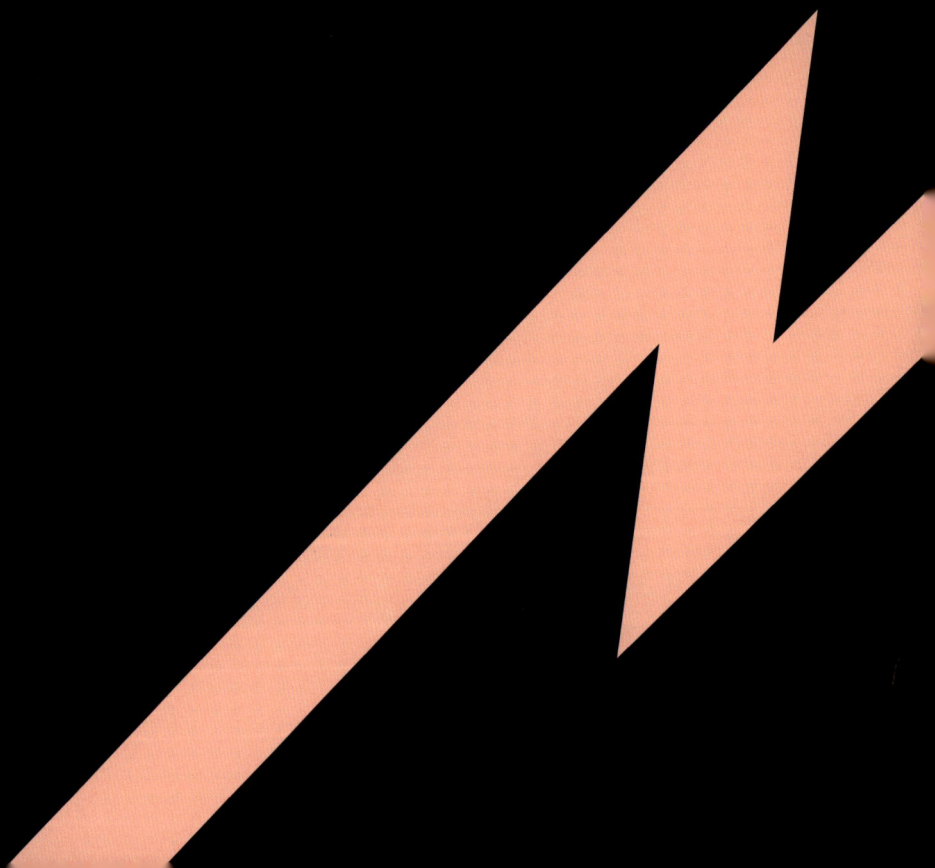

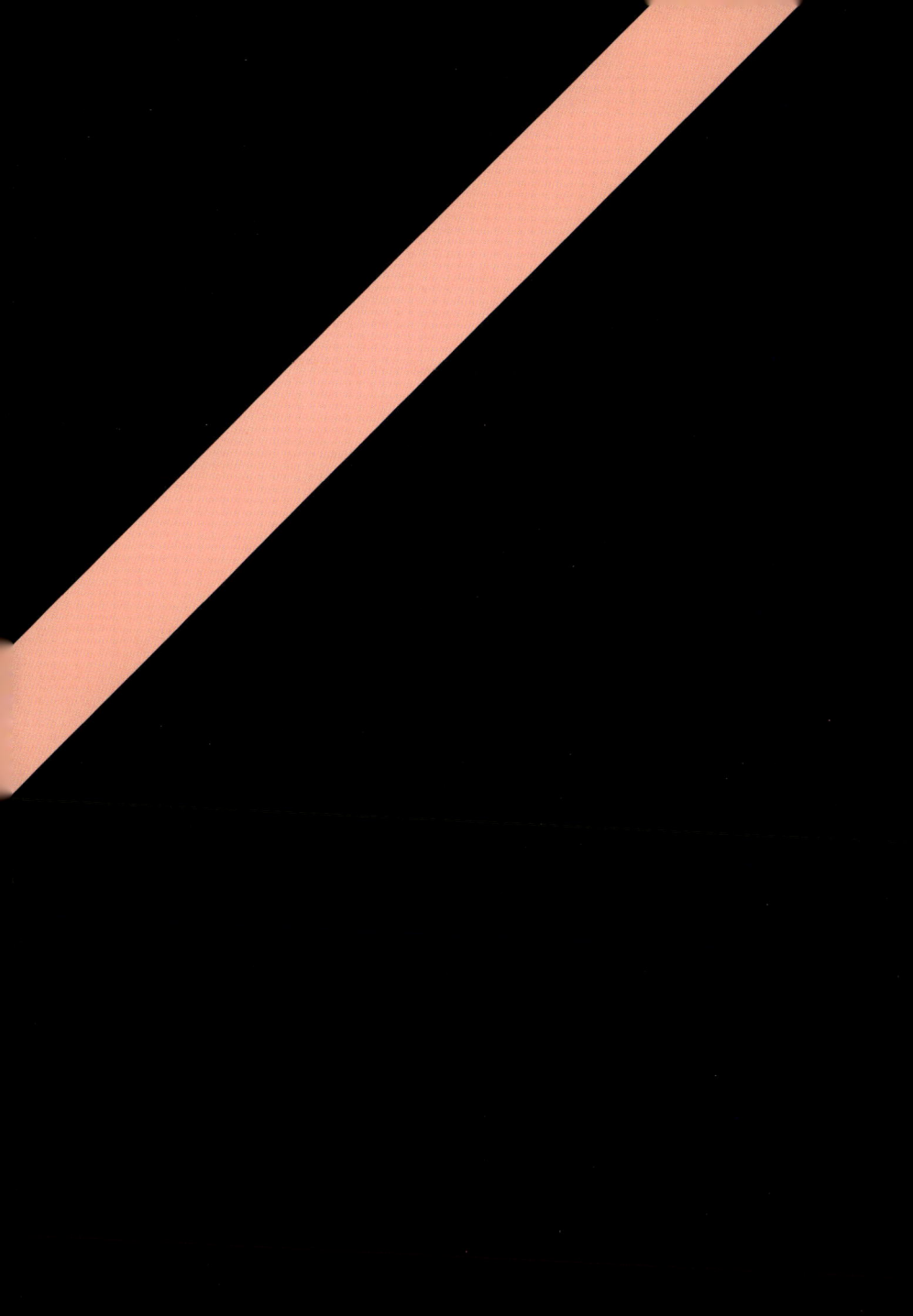

"I've been wearing leather for decades. You can make it look really sexy: I like wearing a leather jacket with a little bustier— more biker chick than rock star."

DOLLY PARTON

*L*ike everything in life, Dolly very much does leather her way, and has worn it throughout her career in various guises, including the rather fetching blue, cinch-waisted leather coat that her character wore in *9 to 5*, which was flared to the knee and was made by the Western Costume Co. Like most of the film's looks, its flavor was a little more demure than the real-life Dolly, who prefers a slightly more heart-racing approach to leather. This is why her archive contains several "cowgirl" outfits—the definition of "spunky" by anyone's standards. While these looks borrowed elements from Western, with details like fringe, rivets, and embroidery, they also had feminine swagger that was all Dolly.

For an appearance on *Austin City Limits*, a program that's been dedicated to showcasing every musical style from country to rock to bluegrass since 1975—hosting heavyweights like Willie Nelson, Emmylou Harris, and Etta

James to name a few—Robért Behar designed a very fitting outfit: a leather vest that had a collar embellished with roses and rhinestones, a fringed skirt and a pink silk shirt, with a pair of suns on each sleeve. It was a tribute to Rose Maddox, a famous country singer who was born in 1925 and an early heroine of Dolly's, and it put forward an alternative set of characteristics for leather that was very Dolly.

Fitted, feminine, and a little flirtatious. That's how leather should look according to Dolly. And on a 1989 episode of *Saturday Night Live*, she ticked all three boxes thanks to Tony Chase, who designed a corseted leather jumpsuit that had swathes of studs at the knees, the waist, and the shoulders. On her feet were a pair of cowboy boots with similarly fabulous hardware adorning each toe.

HOW TO FIND A LEATHER JACKET THAT SUITS YOUR PERSONALITY

A leather jacket is something of a shapeshifter, and can become something minimalist or maximalist depending on the number of zippers, the collar, the fit, or the character of the material itself. But how do you find "the one," so to speak? Because if you do, it's something that will stay in your wardrobe for decades and will just keep getting better with age.

At one end of the spectrum you've got the blouson, a very simple leather jacket that has a boxy silhouette and a single zipper from neck to waist that closes the collar. It's often worn oversized so that the sleeves are ever-so-slightly too long and the hem stretches an inch or so over the hip bone. At the other end, you've got the classic biker, a more detailed jacket that probably has plenty of hardware, zippers, pockets, and maybe even a belt toward the lower hem that can be unbuckled so that it hangs loose. This is probably the most "Dolly" option. It's definitely the sexier choice, as it's designed to sit close to the skin with a much snugger fit than the blouson, which is straight up and down. Of course, if you like the details but not the glove-fit, you can always size up so that your jacket sits on the roomy side. This isn't so Dolly, who always prefers clothes that cleave to the body, but it's a relaxed take on the leather jacket that will work incredibly hard in your wardrobe, because you can wear it with everything from slip dresses, to straight-leg jeans, to smart wool pants for work.

Dolly hasn't worn a moto jacket to my knowledge—a leather jacket with a high collar that's often panelled to look a bit like a race car driver's uniform, with go-faster stripes down the sleeves—but she definitely has the chutzpah to pull one off. As the patron saint of embellishment, another thing that she would probably appreciate is any jacket with fringe, studs, or motifs, as well as a jacket with a statement color like gold, silver, or even red.

EXPANDING THE LEXICON OF LEATHER . . .

There's obviously more to leather than jackets—there are leather skirts and leather pants, leather dresses and leather coats. And Dolly's worn them all. At 2003's Mark Twain Prize, which honored her former co-star and friend Lily Tomlin, the singer gave leather a good name, turning up in a sexily proportioned two-piece that was comprised of a leather vest and a leather skirt. A generous number of studs gave the whole look a bit of a country edge. And it was quite a look, especially when styled with her signature mule sandals; indeed, it was a very convincing argument for why the leather jacket shouldn't always be allowed to hog the limelight.

A leather vest can be a very cool proposition, especially if you buy one that has a single-breasted silhouette (vintage shops will have plenty of decent options in black and brown). You could wear it buttoned up by itself when it's warm enough for bare arms, or you could slip it over a white tee if you want a bit more coverage. Dolly styled her leather vest over a white shirt, which you could also replicate with either a cream pussycat-bow blouse or a silk-charmeuse shirt so that some softness or shine creates a nice contrast with the leather.

A leather skirt is something you may very well already own. And if you don't, you should know that it's something of a workhorse. It will literally go with everything in your wardrobe, especially if it's black and A-line, and it is so easy—just slip on, zip up, and feel polished. Dolly's leather skirt finished about half a foot above her knee, which is a length that works particularly well on petite frames like hers, but experiment with midis and maxis, by all means, as they can look a little more effortless.

Whatever you choose, Dolly's approach to leather was very often dressed up. So while you might be used to wearing your skirt with sneakers or your jacket with jeans, it might be time to dial up the drama. Why not button your vest over a crushed silk dress the next time you're heading out-out? Or pair the lived-in leather jacket you've had for a decade with some rhinestone jeans? Don't be boring when you could be more Dolly.

FIND
POWER
IN PRINT

"You kind of have to be careful how you do a lot of prints or a lot of bold things, because I'm better not to have a whole bunch of that . . . because there's not a whole bunch of me."

DOLLY PARTON

On the back cover of *New Harvest . . . First Gathering*, Dolly's eighteenth solo album, released in 1977, the singer is hailing a cab in New York—the index finger of her left hand is stuck out, as well as her thumb, and she has a megawatt smile on her face. Although David Gahr's original photograph is in black and white, you can see that her dress, which flared out from the hip and finished just above the ankle, incorporated panels of floral material that gave the whole look a girlish aspect. This was something of a transitional moment in Dolly's wardrobe. Just like her sound, which would soon undergo a somewhat controversial shift to include pop songs on her albums, as well as country songs, she was seeking new ways to be "her" while also appealing to a wider audience than ever before. Although this dress's flowing silhouette would ultimately be replaced with something more fitted as she moved into the eighties, Dolly never left print behind. Just like country music, she took print with her as her career evolved.

In fact, some of her most glamorous outings have included a splash of print—the louder, the better, like her leopard-spotted outfit on the cover of *Backwoods Barbie*. Dolly often wore pieces that weren't made with printed fabric, but were rather patterned with embellishment. For 2000's ACM Awards, Dolly wore a hot pink dress by Robért Behar (who also designed her look for *Backwoods Barbie*), which was sewn with clusters of beads to create shimmering leopard spots as soon as they were hit by the stage lights.

She certainly doesn't play by the rules when it comes to prints. In 2014, Dolly performed on the *Today* show, arriving in a three-piece outfit that was spotted *and* striped, as well as being heavy with fringes of beads that shook as she responded to an audience member by wiggling her hips and shouting, "Oh, you like the pants?" The fact that she clashed two prints so effortlessly proved one thing definitively: Dolly doesn't suffer fools who say that spots and stripes don't go together, and, as with everything else, she will wear patterns just how she pleases.

Dolly also relies on print for more down-to-earth moments that don't require a "stage" outfit. When posing for pictures in Dollywood, her widely successful theme park in Pigeon Forge, East Tennessee, Dolly has worn everything from a puff-sleeved dress covered in tiny polka dots, to a plaid shirt with a studded collar. Tony Chase also made her the cutest gingham dress, with puffed sleeves and rickrack detailing, for the cover of her live album *Heartsongs: Live from Home*, which came out in 1994. You get the feeling that this dress is the kind she would have liked to wear as a little girl in the mountains, with its frills and flirtatious length, and, in fact, it looks rather like a dress worn by one of the most famous country stars of all time, Kitty Wells, just with a different print pattern. (Porter Wagoner once compared the two women, rather in favor of Kitty Wells. Bristling about Dolly's appearance in *Playboy*, he commented to the *Tennessean*: "Do you think Kitty Wells would do that?" Dolly's response, many years later in an interview with *Vanity Fair*, was typically Dolly: "I'm *not* Kitty Wells.")

While print can be intimidating for first-timers, it's an easy way to add a sense of playfulness into your wardrobe. And playfulness should be high on your agenda if you want to dress like Dolly.

THE PATTERN INDEX

FLORALS

Dolly wasn't a traditional "florals" kind of person, but she did wear a rose-printed jacquard dress on the cover of *My Blue Ridge Mountain Boy* (1969), reclining on a sofa, biting a fingernail in contemplation. It was a demure look that was very much in keeping with her wardrobe during the days of *The Porter Wagoner Show.*

STRIPES

Five years later, on the cover of *Jolene*, Dolly's blue-and-white striped jumpsuit is the second thing you notice after her pile of gleaming blonde hair.

POLKA DOTS

Red is one of Dolly's favorite colors, and for the cover of *All I Can Do* (1976), she wore a polka-dot shirt that was as sweet as a ripe strawberry.

GINGHAM

Gingham was a go-to for Dolly, especially the red-and-white checks she wore for *Heartsongs: Live from Home*, as well as in the artwork for *Backwoods Barbie*.

PLAID

A favorite of country stars such as Rose Maddox, a plaid shirt was given star billing on the cover of *Run, Rose, Run*.

LEOPARD

Dolly only wore leopard print occasionally, but when she did, it was a traffic-stopping event.

FINDING YOUR FAVORITE PRINT

As you already know, Dolly wore all types of print, from leopard spots to stripes. But if you're new to print, and generally prefer the safety of solid colors, it can be hard to know where to start. First, don't force yourself to get on first-name terms with, say, florals if they're the opposite of your style personality. Instead, ease yourself in, choosing pieces that you wouldn't necessarily class as "printed" to get a feel for what's you and what isn't; for example, you could try a handbag made of snake-printed leather. These are easy to come by at department stores and, although they're at the very subtle end of the print spectrum, will give you a taste of walking on the ever-so-slightly wilder side.

Another good starting point is navy-and-white stripes, which you might already have in your wardrobe in the form of a long-sleeved Breton shirt. You could try a striped print on what's known as a "half-zip" sweater (so-called because of its high neck that can be unzipped to create a large collar), which is another easy style to work into your rotation. Since we're channeling Dolly, my advice would be to buy a size down so that it's fitted enough to tuck into the waistband of your jeans, and wear it with knee-high boots (and if the boots are snake-print, even better).

Once you've got a feeling for what suits you, it's just about how much print you actually want to wear. Leopard print is one that can be statement or subtle. Dolly wore it head to toe thanks to a set of heavily embellished dresses made by Tony Chase, which created the effect of twinkling leopard spots that were truly va-va-voom. But it's also possible to wear leopard print as part of your everyday wardrobe, via jeans, sneakers, loafers, or even a blazer. Dolly also wore the print as a leopard slip dress for *Backwoods Barbie*, which is such an easy style during the summer—low effort but high impact.

Speaking of summer, some prints are more primed for hot weather than others—and gingham is definitely one of them. The shops will be filled with wall-to-wall gingham dresses as soon as it's spring, and, as long as you're a dress person, you'll be able to find one that suits your style. Dolly would choose something feminine and flouncy, with puffed sleeves, or a cinched waist, or ties at the shoulders, or a ruffled hem (or a combination of all of these). But it's also possible to find a gingham dress that doesn't have much in the way of bells and whistles, such as shirtdresses that hit somewhere below the mid-calf, or a simple pinafore-style dress with an empire silhouette that's so easy to wear.

And we can't not mention plaid. My favorite way to wear a plaid shirt—oversized and unbuttoned over a white tank top with straight-legged jeans—could easily be "Dollified"—just add some vertiginous mule sandals. Find out more about those particular shoes—and how to wear them with attitude à la Dolly—in the next chapter.

Print is such an easy way to add excitement to your wardrobe—giving any outfit some look-twice appeal—that it would be a shame not to give it a go at some point or another. The most important thing to remember is that if it *feels* right, it'll look right.

GET A PAIR OF HEELS THAT'S "YOU"

"I loved high heels before I knew I was even gonna be short!"

DOLLY PARTON

*A*s a little girl growing up in the shadow of the Great Smoky Mountains, Dolly Parton was very much aware of high heels—and their particular brand of allure. As well as poring over pages of shoes in catalogs, she would dig through boxes of donated clothes—along with everyone else in her mountain community—hoping to find heels. (She once did, a thrillingly red pair, and insisted they would fit despite others telling her she was too little.)

If, back then, she could have seen herself a decade later, boy would she have been tickled by the shoes that she would accumulate from shops like Frederick's of Hollywood. Because, just like the towering wigs, the constellations of rhinestones, and the acrylic nails, high heels have not just become part of her persona, but part of her very mythology. Even in the early days of *The Porter Wagoner Show*, Dolly was already wearing heels, even though her outfits were relatively conservative for the country

music show's family audience—sixties shift
dresses that looked positively girlish with her
sculpted beehive and, initially, a modest pair of
heels. Toward the end of her seven-year stint
on the show—and certainly once she'd
departed after something of a creative
falling-out with her boss Wagoner—the heels
only got higher. Even on the album covers
where she's dressed down—like her
"handywoman" outfit of a shirt tied at the waist
and flared jeans on *9 to 5 and Odd Jobs* (1980)
—she's wearing an impressively stacked heel. I
imagine she feels quite naked without them.
And in fact, she admitted to wearing what you
might call "house" heels to RuPaul, who
interviewed her in 2020 for *Marie Claire*.
"They're not always as high as the ones I wear
for show. But I'm little. I'm short. And I have to
wear heels in order to reach my cabinets,"
she said.

As well as wanting to give her frame as much of a boost as possible—with heels at one end and hair at the other—Dolly has simply always loved a shoe that gives its wearer stature. And whatever your personal history with heels, you can't deny that they inevitably make you walk a little differently. Even if they're not a part of your everyday wardrobe, and are more part of your once-in-a-blue-moon wardrobe, that's fine. Dolly's preference for heels can still be worked into your "shoedrobe." And if you're so inclined, the good news is that even a low heel can make what you're wearing look more purposeful.

The golden rule when it comes to choosing heels, plain and simple, is to avoid styles that make your toes curl just by looking at them. Comfort is key. Remember that piece of advice, and the world of heels is your oyster.

MULES

Dolly's favorite heels are surely mules, a backless shoe with an enclosed toe. Her version of mules are sandals, which have a slender strap over the toes and a perilously sloped sole because of the heel. Like her clothes, Dolly doesn't tend to buy her shoes "off the rack." Many of her most elaborate mules were made to specifically fit her feet by Pasquale Di Fabrizio, the legendary shoemaker whose footwear was fabulous with a capital F—encrusted with rhinestones, embroidered with a swathe of twinkling beads, and magnificently high thanks to a heel made of Lucite.

Dolly's mules quite literally carried her into what could be called her "high-glam" era—and she hasn't stopped wearing them since the eighties, when often they'd match her bedazzled outfits by Tony Chase. (In pictures of her clothing archive, which was painstakingly created and cared for by her childhood best friend and personal assistant Judy Ogle, you can see row upon row of mules that have been cataloged by color. It's quite something.) They aren't the easiest shoes to wear, especially if they're as lofty as Dolly's, but there's something about a mule.

Spicier than a slingback, cooler than pumps, you really shouldn't knock it until you've tried it. If you're looking for comfort as well as sex appeal, the key is to look for a block heel and a thicker strap across your foot.

A mule can quickly lose its cool factor if you wear it with something that looks too "done." Dolly can slip hers on with second-skin pants to celebrate fifty years of the Grand Ole Opry. That's fine, she's Dolly. But if you try wearing the same combination to the bar? Unfortunately, the effect might not be quite so iconic. So instead, let yours be the star of the show, pairing them with something lo-fi like a white shirt, leather pants, and a plaid blazer.

MULE SANDALS

Oversized denim jacket	Blazer	Faux-fur jacket	High-neck blouse
★	★	★	★
Long-sleeved top	Crewneck sweater	Denim shirt	Knife-pleat pants
★	★	★	★
Box-pleated skirt	Straight-leg jeans	Denim midi skirt	Gold earrings

COWBOY BOOTS

Dolly was more country than Western, but that didn't stop her making cowboy boots one of her signatures. In 1992, she made one of several appearances on *The Oprah Winfrey Show*, performing three songs from the soundtrack of *Straight Talk* (1992), her fifth film. Dolly was wearing a relatively muted outfit by her standards—a red bolero jacket, black leggings, and one of her feathery wigs—but its kicker was a pair of cowboy boots that were distinctly "Dollified." Designed to perfectly coordinate with her jacket, they were cherry red, spike-heeled, and cut with a plunging scallop—fun, fabulously high, and a fitting plus-one for someone like Dolly.

Dolly is so synonymous with what you might call "big personality" cowboy boots that at an exhibition dedicated to the shoe in 2003 at Colorado's Buffalo Bill Museum, a very special pair was displayed. They were white-and-gold with metallic toe caps and a cursive font on the pull strap that read "Dolly."

Around the same time in London, cowboy boots suddenly became a hot commodity thanks to actor Sienna Miller, who wore hers with white tank tops, denim minis, and bangles, as nineties minimalism gave way to aughties boho. Since then, their popularity hasn't waned in over two decades (Miller still packs hers for the Glastonbury Festival). And whatever your style personality, there's a cowboy boot with your name on it, from traditional suede styles with country flair, to sleek leather versions with a touch of cool. For any fan of Dolly's, a pair of cowboy boots is an easy way to integrate a particular brand of swagger into your wardrobe. There's no such thing as too much—for a 1989 appearance on *Saturday Night Live*, Dolly wore cowboy boots that were decorated to look like peacocks (a nod to NBC's peacock logo), with plumage feathers made of cobalt, emerald, and gold beads. Another pair was optic white, stilettoed to the point of almost being vertical, and was studded with tiny gold pyramids around the welt (the edging that surrounds the upper of shoes like brogues).

These are appropriate if you're Dolly Parton. But if you want something that's hardworking enough to go with everything in your wardrobe, look for a simple black ankle boot with a pointed toe, a slanted heel, and a slender sole. It'll be the best of friends with jeans, flaring skirts, and even pantsuits. If you're feeling bolder and looking for a boot that's more of a showstopper, choose a statement leather like snake print, contrast stitching, something that's patterned with studs—or a combination of all three. A knee-high length is also more head-turning—and arguably more versatile, because you can tuck your jeans inside them to go full Dolly, or wear your jeans untucked so that just the boot's vamp peeks out from more of a kick-flared pair. A squared-off boot toe will also look cooler than a pointed or an almond shape.

Of course, Dolly was wearing her cowboy boots a good few decades before they became fashionable, often pairing them with a matching jacket, as she did on *Oprah*. Bambi Breakstone, a costume designer who worked on shows like *Miami Vice*, famously made the star a powder-blue leather blazer that was embroidered with musical notes, banjos, guitars, and the Smoky Mountains. On her feet were a pair of cowboy boots that also twinkled with a treble clef near the crown. As usual, Dolly's take on the ordinary is pretty extraordinary.

COWBOY BOOTS

Long-sleeved top	White shirt	White prairie dress	Blazer
★	★	★	★
Unbuttoned plaid shirt	Denim maxi skirt	Gold hoop earrings	Fine-gauge turtleneck
★	★	★	★
Straight-leg jeans	Trench coat	Suede handbag	Wide-legged jeans

HOW TO WEAR HEELS

If your comfort zone is having your feet horizontal at all times, the most sensible advice would obviously be to ignore heels altogether. If Dolly Parton was your stylist, however, I'm fairly certain she would soon have you wearing stilettos. And as they're such a staple of hers, I'm here to tell you that there are ways to wear heels even if you normally tend to avoid them.

A Cuban heel is a good starting point. This is a slanted heel of no more than a few inches, and you'll often find them on cowboy boots. Trust me, these are even more comfortable than block heels. So much so, I guarantee that even the most anti-heel among you can get on board with them—plus, they look much more effortless than their spike-heeled cousin, the stiletto.

IF YOU HATE HEELS

Parton was also partial to a wedge. As part of a series of visuals for her album *Backwoods Barbie*, she's perched in a rowboat, fishing rod in hand, wearing a puff-sleeved gingham blouse, denim capri pants, and a pair of studded cork wedges. You actually can't see the shoes in the final shot, but you can see that they were part of the ensemble because of the original sketch by Robért Behar. Now, a wedge involves a not inconsiderable boost in the height department, so they're not for the fainthearted, but they'll also be much gentler on your soles than a stiletto because the pressure is more evenly spread over the bottom of each foot.

Dolly famously keeps all her clothes, shoes, and accessories in mint condition thanks to her archive, which is now presided over by her niece, Rebecca Seaver. So why not take a page out of her book on this occasion and, if you have a pair of wedges lurking at the back of your wardrobe from the early aughties, dig them out.

HOW TO SHOW YOUR SHOES SOME TLC

Dolly's favorite shoes have come in and out of fashion over the years. The mule, which rose to popularity in the seventies, fell slightly out of favor, and then experienced another boom in the aughties. It's precisely because different styles of heel ebb and flow that you should meticulously care for everything you own. A chaotic pile of shoes under the stairs will make it that much harder to whip something out when a particular style comes back around. We can't all have an archive like Dolly's, which is a testament to looking after all your investments so that they don't depreciate in value, but with a little bit of TLC, you can make sure your shoedrobe is kept shipshape.

SUEDE-SPRAYING

Dolly-esque cowboy boots are often made of suede, which is particularly susceptible to rain. Invest in a water-repellent spray, which essentially protects the material from anything the weather might throw at it.

STORAGE SOLUTIONS

Back to that chaotic pile under the stairs. Not only is that kind of storage method going to age your shoes terribly through simple rough and tumble, but it also means a) you're never going to be able to find anything, and b) you're going to gradually forget what you own in the first place. Dolly's mules are lined up according to color, with only one side on display so that she can quickly see everything she owns. If you don't have the luxury of space, one solution is to house each pair separately in see-through plastic shoe boxes that can be stacked up neatly. If you're still limited for space, you can also buy shoe storage trays that are flat enough to slot easily under your bed.

REPAIR SERVICES

Dolly rarely throws anything out, so don't be tempted to simply get rid of a pair of shoes if it's looking worse for wear. Shoe repair services can extend the lifetime of your favorite shoes by several years at the very least.

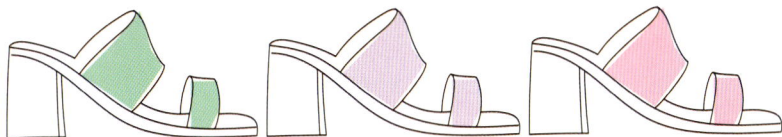

EMBRACE YOUR TASTE

"It takes a lot of time and money to look this cheap, honey."

DOLLY PARTON

*F*rom the very beginning of her career, Dolly was met with opinions about the way she looked from almost everyone she encountered in a professional capacity. From record label executives to reporters who joined her on the road, her appearance was a constant source of intrigue, speculation, and, sometimes, ridicule. In that famous sit-down interview with Barbara Walters in 1977, the same year she went stratospheric with *Here You Come Again*, the journalist rather patronizingly said, in the kind of tone you might use with a child who insists on making the same mistake over and over again: "You don't have to look like this. You're very beautiful. You don't have to wear the blonde wigs. You don't have to wear the extreme clothes, right?" Dolly replied with typical grace: "No, it's certainly a choice."

And it's a choice she made early on. As Dolly has explained in numerous interviews, her look was drawn directly from the sex workers in Sevierville, Tennessee, whose hair, clothes, and makeup were her first introduction to glamour. It was a little girl's impression and one that, interestingly, didn't change even when she was grown. In fact, it was a love that only deepened. "I always liked the look of our hookers back home. Their big hairdos and makeup made them look more. When people say that less is more, I say more is more. Less is less. I go for more," she said during a 1982 interview with *Ladies' Home Journal*.

What's miraculous is that Dolly has managed to hold on to her sense of style—this yearning for "more"—despite fearsome opposition from people, very often men, in positions of power who could effectively make or break her career. When she was signed to Monument Records, its founder, Fred Foster, tried his hardest to mold her in his image. "They wanted to flatten my hair. They wanted me to look more chic and wear more streamlined clothes. He had his assistant take me around, and they set me up with a good hairstylist and a wardrobe person. But I hated everything about it! I felt naked. I might as well have been naked, because they took away my own look," she wrote, recalling the experience in *Behind the Seams*. It was the same story at her next record label, RCA Records, where Chet Atkins, the famous guitarist who became the guiding light of the label's country division in Nashville, also tried to have a gentle word with Dolly, his aim being to coax her out of the fulsome wigs and flamboyant clothes. Obviously, she didn't listen—and also refused to kowtow to the folk at the CMA Awards, who explicitly asked her to wear less hair and makeup. Dolly's reaction was typically Dolly, and she stuck to her guns. As she told the *Tennessean*: "Then I would be like everybody else, and I don't want to be like everybody else. I'm not doing anything to be different. I just don't follow people's trends."

Trends, you see, have never been of interest to Dolly, who only ever wanted to be herself, albeit an enhanced version of herself. Really, it was all a kind of gimmick, a way to draw people in, letting them gawk a little, before the realization would inevitably dawn on them: This woman's got talent. Nothing has stopped her from wearing exactly what she pleases. At 2014's Glastonbury Festival, Dolly delivered a virtuoso performance, wearing an outfit that contained all her hallmarks: a rhinestone vest and spangled pants that looked rather like chaps. As the mistress of country music, she looked 100 percent Dolly.

As she once told William Stadiem, who spoke to the star in 1989 for *Interview*, "When I first started being even more outrageous than I really am, was when people started payin' a lot of attention to me and tellin' me how I should change my hair and the way I dress. And I just thought to myself, not only will I not change it, I'll make it even more exaggerated."

If that isn't a lesson in finding your personal style and sticking with it, I don't know what is.

HOW TO FIND YOUR PERSONAL STYLE

"Style isn't *what* you wear, but *how* you wear it."

"You can buy clothes but you can't buy style."

And, the most cutting of all:

"Style is something you're either born with or you're not."

These are all variations on expressions—clichés, really—that have probably made you feel bad about your personal style at one point or another.

I'm a believer in the school of thought that says if you like something, wear it; if you don't, well, don't wear it. In theory, it's as simple as that, but what can be hard is figuring out what you like. Dolly worked it out very early on, probably because her desire to be a star—and a marketable one who would catch an audience's eye— meant that she had no choice but to make these kinds of decisions from a much younger age than most of us. But it's not easy to be so single-minded as a person moving through the world today. Every day, from morning to night, you're bombarded with information about what you should and—just as importantly—shouldn't be buying. Magazines, social media, group chats—everyone has an opinion about what's "on trend" (as a fashion editor, I plead guilty). But although these can all be useful resources to finding something that feels "you," my best piece of advice is to tune out the background noise as much as possible.

You'll instinctively know what you like, so, first, learn to trust that instinct. Secondly, it's important to move away from the very idea of trends, which can lead to impulse buying

and, ultimately, a lot of disappointment when you realize that you've bought something that has a lifespan of approximately six months. (It goes without saying that a throwaway attitude is proving to be ruinous for the planet.) Instead, your taste should dictate what you purchase—and those purchases should stay in your wardrobe for as long as possible. After all, Dolly keeps denim shirts for decades, archiving all of her clothes so that everything stays in perfect condition.

Of course, there are always turning points in life that might demand something different from your personal style, like starting your first job or leaving your last, which might require a rethink when it comes to your wardrobe. In moments like these, I suggest looking at people whose clothing you admire, and making a mental "mood board"—or even a saved folder on Instagram—so that you can break down the vital stats of their fashion choices. As you'll know by now, Dolly's include embellishment, exaggerated silhouettes, and exuberant colors. Once you've got an idea of a look or a mood, you can then go through your wardrobe, pulling out what still works and spotting any gaps. I'm not suggesting that you periodically bin everything you own—that would be wildly expensive and environmentally irresponsible—but it can be cathartic to systematically resell clothes you aren't wearing so that you're left with a hardworking edit that can better serve your needs.

At the end of the day, Dolly has never taken clothes too seriously. Instead, she's had fun with her wardrobe, and has always stuck to her style principles.

"I ain't in style,
but I like to think I've
got my own style."

DOLLY PARTON

CONCLUSION

Now that you're equipped with these ten style principles, hopefully you're in the mood to dress with a "more is more" attitude, whether that's with a spray of frosted eye shadow, a sprinkling of rhinestones, or both. As long as you feel comfortable in what you're wearing, you're halfway to looking more like Dolly, whose style is more a state of mind than anything else. Dress like the singer who has built a brand around wearing exactly what she pleases, thank you very much. And to the haters, well, you know what to say . . . in the iconic words of Dolly: "Go to hell."

PICTURE CREDITS

Display Quote Sources

Introduction
Fonda, Jane. Quoted in
Dolly Parton: Here I Am.
https://www.bbc.co.uk/programmes/
m000crhq

Wear a Rainbow of Color
Parton, Dolly, *Dolly: My Life and Other
Unfinished Business* (HarperCollins, 1994)

Sculpt Your Silhouette
"Dolly Parton Takes Us 'Behind the Seams'
of Her Unique Style in New Book." *The
View* (October 18, 2023).
https://www.youtube.com/
watch?v=1W0bIdqNIiQ

Embellish to the Nines
Hyland, Veronique, "Dolly Parton May
Look Artificial, but She's Totally Real."
Elle (October 9, 2019).
https://www.elle.com/culture/a29282948/
dolly-parton-jolene-interview-2019/

Dazzle in Denim
Parton, Dolly, *Behind the Seams: My Life
in Rhinestones* (Ten Speed Press, 2023)

Shine in Metallics
Grobel, Lawrence, "The *Playboy*
Interview With Dolly Parton."
Playboy (October 1, 1978).
https://www.playboy.com/read/the-
playboy-interview-with-dolly-parton

Wear "More is More" Hair and Makeup
"Dolly Parton Breaks Down 11 Looks from
1975 to Now | Life in Looks." *Vogue*
(2020). https://www.youtube.com/
watch?v=ohvN75BaY1I

Play with Leather
Parton, Dolly, *Behind the Seams: My Life
in Rhinestones* (Ten Speed Press, 2023)

Find Power in Print
"Dolly Parton Explains the Evolution
of Her Look." *Allure* (2020).
https://www.youtube.com/
watch?v=0PhuSIKwzCQ

Get a Pair of Heels That's "You"
Parton, Dolly. Quoted in BBC's *The One
Show* (July 7, 2023).

Embrace Your Taste
Parton, Dolly, *Dolly: My Life and Other
Unfinished Business* (HarperCollins, 1994)

REFERENCES

Bailey, Jerry, *"Say Hello to the Real Miss Dolly." The Tennessean* (October 20, 1974).

Carson, Johnny, *The Tonight Show.* Interview (1977).

Charles, RuPaul. "Hark! The Herald Dolly Sings." *Marie Claire* (December 7, 2020). https://www.marieclaire.com/celebrity/a34688302/dolly-parton-december-2020-interview/

"Dolly in London: Dolly Parton live in concert at the Dominion Theatre London." HBO (May 21, 1983). https://www.youtube.com/watch?v=WChWz1UZLvQ

"Dolly Parton Answers the Web's Most Searched Questions." *Wired* (October 5, 2020). https://www.youtube.com/watch?v=Bc9gTqiljLA

"Dolly Parton Breaks Down 11 Looks from 1975 to Now | Life in Looks." *Vogue* (2020). https://www.youtube.com/watch?v=ohvN75BaY1I

"Dolly Parton launches new radio show (What Would Dolly Do?) on Apple Music." *TODAY* (October 11, 2023). https://www.youtube.com/watch?v=2cxV5_Wc5rk

Dolly Parton: Here I Am (2019). https://www.bbc.co.uk/programmes/m000crhq

"Dolly Parton performs 'Rockin' at the 2022 Rock & Roll Hall of Fame Induction Ceremony." *Max* (December 1, 2022). https://www.youtube.com/watch?v=eaBVCUIWuSA

"Dolly Parton Says Hello to TODAY: 'I'm as old as yesterday but hopefully as new as tomorrow.'" *Today* (May 13, 2014). https://www.today.com/popculture/dolly-parton-says-hello-today-im-old-yesterday-hopefully-new-2d79658212

Flippo, Chet, "Interview: Dolly Parton." *Rolling Stone* (August 25, 1977). https://www.rollingstone.com/music/music-features/interview-dolly-parton-62625/4/

Grobel, Lawrence, "The *Playboy* Interview with Dolly Parton." *Playboy* (October 1, 1978). https://www.playboy.com/read/the-playboy-interview-with-dolly-parton

Jahr, Cliff, "Golly, Dolly! (What Will She Say Next?)" *Ladies' Home Journal* (July 1982).

Miller, Stephen, *Smart Blonde* (Omnibus Press, 2008).

Parton, Dolly, *Behind the Seams: My Life in Rhinestones* (Ten Speed Press, 2023).

Parton, Dolly, *Instagram* (July 8, 2019). https://www.instagram.com/p/BzqjvS0lpYJ/?hl=en

Parton, Dolly, ed. Randy L. Schmidt, *Not Dumb, Not Blonde: Dolly in Conversation* (Omnibus Press, 2017).

"Porter's Bitter Remarks Turn Dolly's Happiest Hour Sour." *The Tennessean* (October 1978).

Rush, Jeremy, "Dolly Parton: I've Lived So Many Lifetimes." *Goldmine* (December 27, 2002).

Sessums, Kevin, "Good Golly, Miss Dolly!" *Vanity Fair* (June 1991). https://archive.vanityfair.com/article/1991/6/good-golly-miss-dolly

Stadiem, William, "Daisy Mae In Hollywood." *Interview* (July 1989).

Walters, Barbara, Interview on ABC (December 6, 1977).

ABOUT THE AUTHOR

Natalie Hammond is the senior fashion news editor at *Grazia*. She previously worked on the fashion desk at the *Times*, and her writing has appeared in publications including the *Telegraph*, the *Financial Times,* and *gal-dem*. She is also the author of *Style Codes: David Bowie*, and this is her second book.

ACKNOWLEDGMENTS

Thank you to my editors at Ebury, Ru, and Katie, who kept me going every time they popped into my inbox with kind words of encouragement, as well as the most thorough copy editor in the business, Kate. Thank you also to the designer, Claire, and illustrator, Ollie, for their sensitive and inspired work.

To my family, as always, for their belief when my own fails.

And to Dolly, an inspiration to anyone who has ever felt that fashion should be fun. I will always love you.

Editor: Juliet Dore
Design Manager: Danny Maloney
Managing Editor: Jodi Wong
Production Manager: Alison Gervais.

Library of Congress Control Number: 2024943633

ISBN: 978-1-4197-7987-9
eISBN: 979-8-88707-570-9

Printed and bound in China
10 9 8 7 6 5 4 3 2 1

Abrams books are available at special discounts when purchased in
quantity for premiums and promotions as well as fundraising or
educational use. Special editions can also be created to specification. For
details, contact specialsales@abramsbooks.com or the address below.

ABRAMS The Art of Books
195 Broadway, New York, NY 10007
abramsbooks.com